PASQUALE VERDICCHIO

ESSAYS ON HIS WORKS

T0170672

ESSENTIAL WRITERS SERIES 54

Canada Council   Conseil des Arts
for the Arts   du Canada

ONTARIO ARTS COUNCIL
CONSEIL DES ARTS DE L'ONTARIO
an Ontario government agency
un organisme du gouvernement de l'Ontario

Canada

Guernica Editions Inc. acknowledges the support of the Canada Council
for the Arts and the Ontario Arts Council.
The Ontario Arts Council is an agency of the Government of Ontario.
We acknowledge the financial support of the Government of Canada.

PASQUALE VERDICCHIO

ESSAYS ON HIS WORKS

Edited by Antonio D'Alfonso

GUERNICA
EDITIONS
TORONTO-CHICAGO-BUFFALO-LANCASTER (U.K.)
2020

Antonio D'Alfonso, editor
Michael Mirolla, general editor
Joseph Pivato, series editor
Cover design: Allen Jomoc, Jr.
Interior design, typesetting & front cover image: Antonio D'Alfonso
Guernica Editions Inc.
287 Templemead Drive, Hamilton (ON), Canada L8W 2W4
2250 Military Road, Tonawanda, N.Y. 14150-6000 U.S.A.
www.guernicaeditions.com

Distributors:
Independent Publishers Group (IPG)
600 North Pulaski Road, Chicago IL 60624
University of Toronto Press Distribution,
5201 Dufferin Street, Toronto (ON), Canada M3H 5T8
Gazelle Book Services, White Cross Mills
High Town, Lancaster LA1 4XS U.K.

First edition.
Printed in Canada.

Legal Deposit – Fourth Quarter
Library of Congress Catalog Card Number: 2020942166
Library and Archives Canada Cataloguing in Publication
Title: Pasquale Verdicchio : essays on his works / edited by Antonio D'Alfonso.
Names: D'Alfonso, Antonio, 1953- editor.
Series: Essential writers series ; 54.
Description: Series statement: Essential writers ; 54
Identifiers: Canadiana (print) 20200295098
Canadiana (ebook) 20200295195
ISBN 9781771836470 (softcover)
ISBN 9781771836487 (EPUB)
ISBN 9781771836494 (Kindle)
Subjects: LCSH: Verdicchio, Pasquale, 1954-
—Criticism and interpretation.
Classification: LCC PS8593.E692 Z63 2020
DDC C818/.5409 — dc23

CONTENTS

ACKNOWLEDGMENTS

The editor wishes to expresses his deepest gratitude to Kenneth Scambray for having pushed me to bring to fruition the idea on a book of essays of our friend Pasquale Verdicchio's poetry and essays.

Antonio D'Alfonso's essay "The Naïf Nomad" appeared in a diffierent version as the Preface of Pasquale Verdicchio's French-language translation by Antonio D'Alfonso, *Le paysage qui bouge*, Montréal: Éditions du Noroît, 2000.

Leonardo Buonomo's "In the Name of the Farther" was previously published in Buonomo's *From Pioneer to Nomad: Essays on Italian North American writing*, Guernica: 2003.

Laura E. Ruberto's review, *Bound by Distance: Rethinking Nationalism through the Italian Diaspora* by Pasquale Verdicchio, first appeared in *MELUS Journal of the Society of the Multi-Ethnic Literature of the United States*, Issue 26.1 (Spring 2011), pages 259-262. It is reprinted by permission of the journal in its original review style.

Versions of Kenneth Scambray's reviews, "The Dissonant Subject: *Devils in Paradise; Writings on Post-Emigrant Cultures*" and "The Decontextualized Subaltern: *Bound by Distance: Rethinking Nationalism in the Italian Diaspora*", appeared in *L'Italo-Americano*. A version of Scambray's review, "Culture, Identity, and Language in Pasquale Verdicchio's *The House is Past: 1978-1998*", appeared in *The Paterson Literary*, no. 32, pages 257-259. It is reprinted by permission of Maria Mazziotti Gillan, editor of *The Paterson Literary Review*.

An idea for a good book is just an idea until a publisher accepts to print the manuscript. Started decades ago, the Essential Writers Series continues to offer essays, articles, reviews, and interviews written by fellow writers and scholars on contemporary writers. A special thank you to Ken Scambray whose presence was essential in this work. Let us tip our hats to Michael Mirolla and Connie Guzzo-McParland for persevering and forging ahead.

ANTONIO D'ALFONSO

THE NAÏF NOMAD

This coffin ship you call a country has a big hole in it.
Mary Melfi, *Office Politics*

EVERY CULTURE CREATES its literary modus operandi. The notion we have of a country's literature, when fully blossomed, becomes the variable we name tradition. As it often happens with tradition, its rules and regulations are hard to wreck. The person who dares crack open its hard shell rarely comes out of it without reproach. It is during the transcription of culture to which the writer claims to belong, and by respecting the precepts accepted by the literary institutions, that determines what is success or failure. The more the writer follows the codes of style, the permissible contents, the social decorum, the self-censorship, the greater are the chances for the writer of turning into a literary hero. If the writer disturbs, he will be gagged by media silence. Inescapably follow social and literary failure. The scarcity of exceptions proves how inflexible the laws of literature really are. The writer either kisses the hand that feeds him or else he is thrown out of the festivities.

History demonstrates that important contemporaries are the mediocre authors of tomorrow. The writer who might be significant in the future is undoubtedly composing in the tranquility of his room, head bent over a ream of paper, when (s)he is not out strolling down an alley without making a racket. Neither time nor the emerging generation is indulgent in regard to works of the past now out of fashion. Yet there are exceptions. If an author of the past continues to arouse enthusiasm in another era, it is thanks precisely to the fact that we are dealing with an exception, a recusant. Nonconformity confers a particular appeal to the weird, the strange, the deviant, the astonishing, the indefinable, the shady writer.

Not to go with the flow usually leads such a writer to adopt the life of the recluse, and in so doing refuses to publicly voice his opinions. He ends up choosing the road most of his contemporaries are not aware exists. He (this convenient pronoun includes all genders) might even find himself on roads taken by others, but strangely he does not discover what other writers discover. Somehow at some point he goes astray, zigzagging here and there, and does not notice just how far off the track he has gone, and once again grudgingly realizes he is alone, terribly alone, struck down by ostracism that he himself is responsible for. He knows it. Reluctantly he might, like Kafka, ask one of his friends to destroy all his scribblings once dead. Of course, he suspects that no friend in his right mind would respect such a funereal testament. There is nothing miserable about being humble in front of time.

Purity is annoying; what is pure is never clearly defined. Applied to style, purity looks like mannerism; applied to society, it gives birth to curious laws of exclusion. Despite pluriethnic demographics, English Canada has produced few "strange" works. Many authors privilege established values, using a refined style, and a delicately intelligent syntax; yet readers rarely notice a crack, a hole gaping into a deep sea. This is the mirror of sameness.

If we identify a writer emerging from a cultural minority, we divine the freedom he had to forsake in exchange of recognition. The writer of ethnic background often follows Faust's fate: ready to hand over his soul for a moment of glory. Established writers, however, are neither bureaucrats nor presidents of occult societies.

The fate of silence is not limited to ethnic writers. We simply cannot appreciate writings that derail our sense of taste. We disregard this as being bad literature. Even if translated such works are not permitted access to the tours of national literature. To be established does not mean that the writer is exceptional. Experimentation finds its source outside political borders. Translations become metaphors for distant voices which some translators make their own. Most readers favor the expression of the unconscious of the nation. Individual style of the singular writer walking outside the confines of the expected is sneered at. There is the dark cloud under which Pasquale Verdicchio writes. His room, his workshop, his studio are moving landscapes. Nothing is ever stationary.

Born in Naples, Italy, Pasquale Verdicchio came with his parents and brothers to Vancouver in the 1960s. Like many Italian children living in Canada, he attended English-language schools, not speaking a word of English. He spoke Neapolitan and Italian at home. When he began to compose his texts he decided to translate the after-World-War-II poets of Italy, in particular the Novissimi, who, in his mind and heart, represented a safe haven for the complex young emigrant he was. His essential rupture consisted of realizing he was a person without a home anywhere.

Inescapably Pasquale identified with writers who deconstructed their working instrument: language. Unlike writers who, like him, experienced the trauma of emigration, Pasquale doggedly declined to be huddled by nostalgia. Be it only on this precise point, he radically distanced himself from the work produced by fellow emigrant writers. There was no way back home, to paraphrase him. There was no lost paradise behind him. He began at zero. His writings are presented like the first words uttered by a child: everywhere new horizons appeared. Yet too few noticed these undiscovered territories.

When we open a poetry book by Pasquale we are immediately struck by the recurrences of ellipses. The reader frequently trips over phrases that seem incomplete; his broken sentences are offensive on their structural level. To attribute intentions of expressly wanting to displease — which Pasquale never wanted to do — would be inappropriate, if not outright distasteful. He writes like he lives. His poems reflect the scattered existence of people seasoned in worldliness. If this familiarity with the unknown upsets some readers, if his observations on the future discompose, since most readers presume to find *topoi* — stereotypical images of immigration — in ethnic writers, it is simply because Pasquale takes nothing for granted and must invent his raw material. Uneasiness forbids him to embrace blindly the very stuff of his craft. To claim that his writing seems laborious would be to rebuke much of twentieth century literature. We speak badly because we live badly.

Readers have not always been kind to Pasquale's books. They attack him for not knowing how to write. Some even reckon that he might be better served if he wrote in Italian. Pasquale is not an Italian-language poet; he is an English-language poet, but his idiom is an Italian blanket he drops over the shoulders of non-English readers. His verse halts half way. If there are images in this poetry, as we should assume to meet in all poetry, they are here torn to bits, cropped, the same way some famous painter would rip apart his famous painting. Meaning is there, in the gesture, no doubt about it, but the reader must now glue the pieces back together. Many reviewers might be tempted to compare this sort of writing to deconstructive writing and L=A=N=G=U=A=G=E poetry, but to do so would be misleading. On the surface a Verdicchio text might share common aspects with practitioners of such literary currents: the poet no longer trusts language as being the primary raw matter. Pasquale would be the first to acquiesce to the affinities. But to advance the obvious is too easy an answer for a rather complex question.

Formal experiments overlap in some instances, intersect like the circles in Venn diagrams. Viewed from another angle, however, the watchful reader will discern how these literary orbits are located on separate planes, each layer rotating in their respective directions.

Modernist texts emerged from a desire to transform the assumptions of language, even if this entails the destruction of language. Modernists reduce idiom to its smallest constituents in order to better control their sense; they might even want to displace meaning History poured into terms, as Feminist writers have done. Men and women who have reached the finish line of their particular cultural journey invented Modernity. Modernity is a consequence, an end result, the final curtain, beyond which point metamorphosis hopefully begins. I say hopefully because there was a tendency in modernist poets to assert their contributions as providing permanent significance. What

Pasquale Verdicchio calls attention to is the fact such an enterprise should not aim at acclamation, but at nobility of spirit. Big words, but how else to name Pasquale's unique venture of formal displacement?

Writing as practiced by Pasquale is not the crowning glory bestowed on a winner or finalist. His is engagement, commencement, risk, and speculation. Not post-modernity, but a gambit: a sacrifice for a possible greater advantage. His apparent awkwardness is a skill; his imperfections, pursuits. Like the infant, like the emerging writer, like the elderly learning a new trade. Every single undertaking is a program. Modernity caters to those with the talent for language. Without modernity, there would be no Pasquale Verdicchio, we all agree.

He acknowledges the craftsmanship and the accomplishments of the movement, confesses to borrowing and stealing from their well. In truth, Pasquale writes like a Sunday artist paints. I consider him a naïf writer, who feigns ignorance, who pretends not knowing a thing about poetry. He is a master of disguise. Those bits of sentences and phrases that stop before the end are not confetti cast to an audience waiting to be surprised. Remember, these are neither the products of affectation, nor the devices of a magician. The stakes are always extremely high.

Pasquale's lyricism is not romantic, not postmodernist. Manifestation of emotion is abrogated; idiomatic expressions dyslexic; inversions never puns.

Idiom is not mastered intentionally. Pasquale's poem is not versified prose. He doesn't want to rehash a story. Even when he tells a tale, he misplaces the punch line. No pretty lines, no ugly sentiments. No rational emotional, no unreal world. There is the earth shifting, there is a traveller who crosses over moving landscapes, territories where vocabularies lose their meaning as soon as they are uttered.

According to Pasquale Verdicchio, the task of the poet is to disclose global unconsciousness and to poke at the mechanisms of false probity. And no solution remedies the troubles that ensue. No language can be trusted. No emotion is self-sufficient. No concept totally accurate. Pasquale spreads open the fissure between word and word, between culture and culture.

Fragments are queries sent to readers who are not always receptive. His verse is unstitched, his imagery blurry, phrases offer no plot to follow out to easy meanings, his score stays clear of surrealism and the tightrope daredevils of automatist writing. His sentences are presented like mathematical formulae. As is made clear by the titles Pasquale Verdicchio gives his poetry books — *Moving Landscape, Nomadic Trajectory, Approaches to Absence,* and *This Nothing's Place* — he is fascinated by drifting, shuffling, relocation. The world is changing, altering us all, and requires that we move along with it. Pasquale Verdicchio is a nomad stepping from one plane onto another, whose identity fluctuates: Italian, he writes in Canadian; Canadian, he writes in American; English, he writes in Neapolitan. He writes in a dialect that is an international language. Labels are heavy burdens, and the poet should dodge banners and flags. Pasquale Verdicchio has built a house floating through space at record speeds.

GIULIANA GARDELLINI

THE DYNAMICS
OF MEMORY

Look. Have No Words.
Pasquale Verdicchio

A POETIC TEXT is a limited and well-circumscribed entity: its beginning and its end, as well as the shape and the borders of its typographic characters, are delimited by the white of the page, which confines it to the status of a detached monad. These restrictions can bring about a sense of frustration and claustrophobia stifling the reach of poetic inspiration. In this light, the poetry of Pasquale Verdicchio could be viewed in terms of a titanic effort to defy and overcome, at once, both the limits of language and those of writing. The *monadism* of the written poem is challenged by the *nomadism* of his poetic inspiration, which moves back and forth in place and in time to ideally reach a freedom of expression that the constraints of form seem to deny.

In "A Poet in a Moving Landscape", an interview with Dino Minni, Verdicchio asserted that "[t]o write is to migrate, to be in constant movement" (135), an affirmation which does obviously clash with the fixity and the limitedness of the written text. Verdicchio's poetry offers a way out of what would seem to be an unabridgeable dichotomy: each of his poems is a fragment of poetic diction which, by virtue of its intratextual and intertextual references, flings the reader out of itself, encouraging him/her to explore the sources and the allusions suggested. Verdicchio's poetry is intentionally laconic, full of ambiguities and blanks; it suggests more than it actually says, by hinting at a plurality of meanings which call for multifarious interpretations.

Literary criticism, especially in the 1970s and 1980s, has been dominated by the debate about Postmodernism. In the Anglo-Saxon domain, Postmodernism has often been described as an enormous container of disparate literary experiences, which have in common a few features: the decentralisation of the text and of the author; the fragmentation of the text, of language and of the author's identity; parody and irony; a conflicting attitude towards history and literary tradition; metatextuality. Although Verdicchio's poetry reflects most of these characteristics, for the sake of this discussion I will concentrate in particular on the issue of fragmentation in which, I argue, the dynamics of memory is deeply rooted.

Each poem, far from being a comprehensive text, is presented as a fragment, a piece of poetic inspiration which occasionally takes form on the written page. It has no claim to all-inclusiveness: a poet of postmodernity, Verdicchio is fully aware of the fact that any literary exercise is, by its own nature, limited in scope. His poetic fragments, though, are the literary manifestations of moments of being, where time is not *chronos* but *kairòs*, where the instant is more important than the flux, where the story is less important than the episode. A story can be told in different ways, but always moves on the line of *chronos*; it expands in surface, but not in depth; it moves in a horizontal sense from the beginning to the end, taking the reader by the hand through the acknowledged paths of logical connections of events. Verdicchio is not interested in this narrative device. The motion of his intellect, as well as of his poetic inspiration, is vertical, in the sense of depth. References to the reality outside the text are limited to a few hints aimed more at suggesting than at describing, because it is by moving innerward, in the maze of human conscience, that what really matters can be discovered.

Samuel Beckett, in his essay on Proust, wrote that "[t]he only fertile research is excavatory, immersive, a contraction of the spirit, a descent. The artist is active, but negatively, shrinking from the nullity of extracircumferential phenomena, drawn in to the core of the eddy" (*Proust* 65-6).

If Beckett's poetics casts a special light on Verdicchio's work, Proust is also an important reference, especially as far as the concept of time is concerned. Time, "that double-headed monster of damnation and salvation," as Beckett defined it, is to Proust not an outer dimension, but an inner one (*Proust* 11). Time is a subjective entity, inasmuch as the concept of duration, in a Bergsonian sense, refers to the perception of the time-flow by the individual conscience. And this is precisely what happens in Verdicchio's poetry: the text is a patently subjective entity, in which the reader is given clue upon clue to enter its dynamics and participate in the poetic composition, by subsuming the temporal dimension of the poet, the *kairòs* of his individual conscience. At this stage, the reading process becomes intriguing.

As Verdicchio writes in "The Arsonist", "[i]t doesn't take long to realize that all the lines become one. A continuous following and return. Any point becomes the starting place and eventually represents the end. There isn't much one can do when faced with the aggressive confluence of points" (*Nomadic Trajectory, The House Is Past* 86).

The points the poet speaks of are, to use an astronomical metaphor, white dwarfs, lumps of meaning towards which all the outer elements lead. Verdicchio's idea of contraction, moreover, could be said to be the literary parallel of Wassily Kandinsky's conception of painting. As a matter of fact, to Kandinsky, the point represents the greatest possible reticence in pictorial expression:

The geometrical point is an invisible being. It therefore must be defined as immaterial. From a material point of view the point equals Zero. But this Zero hides several "human" characteristics. In our conception this Zero — the geometrical point — evokes absolute concision, that is to say, the greatest reticence, but which nevertheless speaks. Thus the geometrical point in our conception is the ultimate and unique union of silence and word (Kandinsky, quoted by Verschaffel and Verminck 126).

Verdicchio's poetry is written on the threshold of silence, of the annihilation of language. His relationship to language is undoubtedly conflicting: if, on the one hand, language is the expressive tool that allows him to give voice to his inspiration, on the other, it is a treacherous device that impairs pure poetic diction. In "What Are Clouds?", Verdicchio speaks of the "murderous hand of language" (*The Posthumous Poet, The House Is Past* 103). In "Baptism", which is included in *Terra Mara*, language is described as "a bodily function / that cannot be washed away" (*The House Is Past* 138). Finally, in "Postscript", language is said to change "on the way from mind to mouth", thus failing to express what originally was intended (*The House Is Past* 162). This attitude towards language is reminiscent, in some respects, of Beckett's poetics of the "unword": "As we cannot eliminate language all at once, we should at least leave nothing undone that might contribute to its falling into disrepute. To bore one hole after another in it, until what lurks behind it — be it something or nothing — begins to seep through; I cannot imagine a higher goal for a writer today" (Letter to Axel Kaun, *Disjecta* 172).

In Verdicchio's poetry, many metapoetic lines overtly undermine the status of language. Language, in its material manifestations, is reputed insufficient to get to the core of the matter. This is the reason why, in "Winter Insect, Summer Grass", the poet yearns for "*what exists prior to / the division of meaning*", presumably "Language" with a capital "L", which would obliterate all the distinctions of national belonging for the sake of expressiveness (*The House Is Past* 71). As a matter of fact, in his essay "The Failure of Memory in the Language", Verdicchio writes that "[t]he world is much too multifaceted for any one language, and to find an adequate expression for the totality of things in language is an impossibility" (*Devils* 96). Being bilingual, as Verdicchio is, is therefore an invaluable advantage for a poet, in that it gives him/her a wider range of expressive choices to be exploited in the act of composition.

Verdicchio's poetics of the fragment and his views on language are, in my opinion, the necessary premises for a discussion of the dynamics of memory in his poetry, in that they make it work in a way that is different from many other Italian-Canadian writers. In a recent interview by Antonio Maglio published in *Tandem*, Verdicchio said that "[t]he presence of nostalgia in our community is not always negative. If it is only sentimental and emotional languor, of course it becomes a limiting factor. But if nostalgia becomes curiosity, an effort to understand what's in one's chromosomes, then it can be welcome." Indeed, in Verdicchio's poetry, sentimentalism and "emotional languor" are definitely banned: he never speaks directly or in a "narrative" way of emotional episodes connected either with his family or with the experience of emigration. On the other hand, nostalgia, in its positive meaning, comes to be one of the driving forces of his poetry, in that it leads him to meditate on his roots and on his condition as a man of postmodernity. When asked by Dino Minni whether he deliberately avoided the theme of immigration in his poetry, Verdicchio answered:

> I don't think I deliberately avoid the theme of immigration. I've never really felt an immigrant. I've felt alienated, and yes, a feeling of duality and multiplicity. But such feelings are a natural result of being in some way different; one does not have to be an immigrant to feel like that. There is a state of mind that could be labeled "immigrant" even if one has never emigrated. Even though I don't talk directly about immigration, I am sure that it comes through in my work. I don't think it can be helped (*Devils* 134).

Verdicchio is an immigrant, but not because he emigrated. More than anything, the *topos* of immigration is connected to his being a *déraciné*, a man who belongs to no land, inasmuch as his mind rejects any inclusion or classification. Poetry, though, represents to him a form of insight that allows him to explore the sources both of his self and of his genetic origin. Verdicchio's poetic texts could therefore be viewed in terms of thin diaphragms, which, by osmotically absorbing elements both from the past and from the present of poetic composition, make possible the process of recalling. The past undeniably leaves indelible marks on the individual conscience since, as Beckett observed in his essay on Proust: "[t]here is no escape from yesterday because yesterday has deformed us, or been deformed by us . . . [W]e are other, no longer what we were before the calamity of yesterday" (*Proust* 13). Verdicchio makes no attempt to negate this. The question is, how the process of memory actually takes place. Consistently with the poetics of the fragment, it does not take place in a linear way. Since it is episodic, incomplete, partial and subjective, the process of memory bears the same marks of fragmentariness, which belong to the poetic text itself. Because of the modes by which memory is evoked within the poetic texts, an analogy could be drawn with the dynamics of Proust's involuntary memory, as described by Beckett:

> Involuntary memory is explosive, "an immediate, total and delicious deflagration . . ." [I]t abstracts the useful, the opportune, the accidental, because in its flame it has consumed Habit and all its works, and in its brightness

revealed what the mock reality of experience never can and never will reveal — the real. (*Proust* 13)

In Verdicchio's poetry, memory takes the form of a series of epiphanic visions that allow the poet to bring to light fragments of episodes from his own past. Poems such as "Letter" (from *Moving Landscape*) or "Branta Canadensis" (from *Nomadic Trajectory*) are, in my opinion, good instances of this feature. In the former, a "blue envelope stained by foreign fingers" is the anamnestic fragment that gives the *incipit* to the poem; in the latter, the same function is played by a "mouth full of names before the leaving / people at the open border: / nothing and nothing to fear" (*The House Is Past* 10, 54).

The fragments of images lead the poet's mind, as well as the reader's intellect, to take a route moving both backwards and forwards through time and place. Language is essentialized: logical connections are reduced to a minimum to suggest more through the power of vision than through the power of words.

Verdicchio's poems are texts, in spite of the fact that they persistently deny their own status. The limit to which they tend is a composition whose characteristics be analogous to those of painting: a hermetic, single image that synthesises in itself the whole of the text. The poem ought to be an "unceasing image", "a closed rose, impenetrabile / image of silence — its impact as a whole", which would make it possible "to intuit totality" ("Ariadne: Come and Gone", "Removing Depth" in *Nomadic Trajectory, The House Is Past* 56, 55). Image, therefore, is supposed to be both the source of poetry and its eventual form. For this reason, Verdicchio's poetry could be compared to painting, the words he uses being the linguistic paraphrase of the image conveyed by the strokes of his pen.

As I have tried to demonstrate, memory works hand in hand with the flowing of images. Although these images obviously take on diverse episodic forms, I will restrict my analysis to two recurrent *topoi*: house and displacement. *The House Is Past* groups most of Verdicchio's compositions from 1978 to 1998. The word "house" is denoted as coincident with the word "past", thus establishing the identity between these two concepts. But the past is revisited by the mind of the poet through the images he manages to evoke. The past, as well as the house as a metaphor for familiarity and belonging, is therefore a space where memory is left free to wander and discover sparks of insight. Yet the house is not a narrow box separating the inside from the outside; rather, it is an open container allowing contaminations in both directions.

In "This House, That House" we read: "this is our home, / where we live without windows, / no door to stand behind; / walls and roof unexpected / (the key does not exist, / hanging from a nail behind the door / the word open on the wall)" (*Ipsissima Verba, The House Is Past* 27). The existence of the house as an abstract concept sounds reassuring, insofar as it provides an ideal point of reference to the poet who, on the other hand, "keep[s] running and running", because his roots are everywhere in the "critical geography" he recreates from the places of his memory (*The House Is Past* 27, 117).

"[O]bsessed with displacement," as Verdicchio writes in "The Visible Man", he conceives life, as well as writing, as a constant process of migration, of motion from one place to another (*Isthmus*, *The House Is Past* 48). This *nomadism* is an effective tool to discard the *monadism* of a traditional conception of literature too narrowly stifled within the strict borders of canon and of national belonging. Verdicchio has actually resided in many different places in his life, but real motion is not essential in order to be a nomad, because "[t]he nomad is he who does not move," as he himself asserts in the exergue of "Between the Desert" (from *Nomadic Trajectory*, *The House Is Past* 73). Being a nomad means to be in constant exile from every place and from oneself; paradoxically, the nomad is present in his absence, in the subtraction of himself from a space. Being here or anywhere else eventually makes no difference, since, as Verdicchio asserts in "A Critical Geography", "[m]emory situates and deforms space / lays down its bearings / all based on a sketchy identity / attempt at continuity" and, later, "all paths back from / one direction or the other they cross / where a black feather falls" (*Approaches to Absence*, *The*

House Is Past 117, 118). And, again, in "Between the Desert", we read that "[e]xile [is] constant / for the nomad / who has every / and no place" (*The House Is Past* 75).

In this poetics of displacement, the house represents a sort of cathedral in the desert, which is eagerly sought, but only to be abandoned after a while. Memory is left free to recall and re-create images of the past and of a state of belonging. The absence of a well-denoted place of reference, or "atopism", as Verdicchio argues in his essay "Writing Out of Tongue" "is a precondition of nomadism. The atopic subject is unrooted and thrives on multidimensional relationships within his environment . . . What remains to be done through re-membering is to arrive at a state in language that is as open as possible at the semantic level. The nomad moves through signs that must constantly be reinterpreted and can never be taken for granted" (*Devils* 110).

A nomad of the atopic space, the poet is also a nomad in the forest of language, thanks to the ability of seeing linguistic signs as fresh and "pure" material to be combined anew. It is by conceiving fragmentary images of a past revisited with the naive eyes of the unrooted present that the nomad/poet can discover his/her own identity. As Antonio D'Alfonso states in his essay "Atopia": "[i]t is clearly in exile that the individual will discover his true identity, and not by consuming the salts of the earth. An individual who knows how to fly lives closer to his identity, than one who crawls in the wet soil of nationhood. Here is the identity that is shared by many and everywhere across the world" (55).

The dynamics of memory in Verdicchio's work — by using images of permanence and displacement which, in turn, urge the surfacing of the past and of personal identity — is ultimately coincident with the dynamics of language in poetic composition. Silence is to language what atopia is to memory. In "Note to Ludwig W.", a prose poem included in *Ipsissima Verba*, Verdicchio clearly alludes to this idea:

The words have entered but there is no trace of them. There cannot be any rejection. The delay is due to the inability to recognize one's own prefix. Thick in definition, gathered around a compass. It will not lead you astray. Look. Have No Words. Keep the spell out of names.

From the word silence to express the movement from letter to letter understood from nothingness preceding and following.

To make one's self unknown through the work of others; sculpting glances that set into a block of air that gradually loses shape and becomes a summer road's response to air.

Probe with one construction another. Not imitation, the thing is — is not always and returns. Touching both edges. One sharp enough to cut off communication.

The eye,
barely seen, enters the field of vision. Backs into itself.
Someone
looking over, no one . . .
and just one last word *(The House Is Past 26)*.

Works Consulted

Beckett, Samuel. *Disjecta*. London: Calder, 1983.

_____. *Proust and Three Dialogues with Georges Duthuit*. London: Calder, 1987.

Boelhower, William, and Rocco Pallone, eds. *Adjusting Sites. New Essays in Italian American Studies*. Stony Brook: Forum Italicum, 1999.

Buonomo, Leonardo. "In the Name of the Farther: The Poetry of Pasquale Verdicchio." *Adjusting Sites*. Ed. W. Boelhower and R. Pallone. 153-61.

_____. "Defining the Self Through Memory: The Poetry of George Amabile and Pasquale Verdicchio." *Memoria e sogno: quale Canada domani?* Proc. of the Tenth International Congress of the *Associazione Italiana di Studi Canadesi*, Venice, May 1994. Ed. G. Marra, A. De Vaucher and A. Gebbia. Venezia: Supernova, 1996. 109-13.

D'Alfonso, Antonio. "Atopia." *Social Pluralism and Literary History. The Literature of the Italian Emigration*. Ed. Francesco Loriggio. Toronto: Guernica, 1996, 48-60.

———. "Le nomade naïf." Preface. *Le paysage qui bouge*. By P. Verdicchio. Ed. and trans. A. D'Alfonso. Montréal: Éditions du Noroît, 2000. 9-16.

Kandinsky, Wassily. *Point et ligne sur plan*. Paris: n.p., 1991.

Loriggio, Francesco, ed. *L'altra storia. Antologia della letteratura italo-canadese*. Vibo Valentia: Monteleone, 1998.

Micarelli, Maria. "*La poesia italo-canadese*." *Canada: testi e contesti*. Ed. Alfredo Rizzardi. Abano Terme: Piovan Editore, 1983. 315-23.

Sanfilippo, Matteo. "Italian Travellers in Canada (19th-20th Centuries). A Bibliographical Outline." *Memoria e sogno*. Ed. G. Marra, A. De Vaucher and A. Gebbia. 354-8.

Verdicchio, Pasquale. *Devils in Paradise. Writings on Post-Emigrant Cultures*. Toronto: Guernica, 1997.

_____. *The House Is Past: Poems 1978-1998*. Toronto: Guernica, 2000.

_____. "Looking for Italy Within Our Communities." Interview with Antonio Maglio. *Tandem. Canada's Cosmopolitan News, Arts and Sports Paper*. 9-16 June 2000. http://www.tandem-news.com/focus.html.

_____. "A Poet in a Moving Landscape." Interview with Dino Minni. *Devils in Paradise*. 131-8.

Verminck, Mark, and Bart Verschaffel, eds. *Wordlessness*. Dublin: The Lilliput Press, 1993.

JOSEPH PIVATO

NO NOSTALGIA

As a Southern Italian e/immigrant, I offer this new translation of *The Southern Question* in the spirit of alliance to groups who are today living the history that the Italian immigrant community seems to have long denied. I also offer it up to Italian immigrants to all parts of the globe as a path through which to revive and acknowledge a neglected history (10).

WITH THESE INTRODUCTORY WORDS from Pasquale Verdicchio's translation of Gramsci's famous essay we see Verdicchio's critical view of history in contrast to the clichés of immigrant nostalgia. This critique of the immigrant narrative begins in his early poetry and continues into his later books. This reading of Verdicchio's poetry begins in an ironic post-colonial common place.

The scene is a predominantly Italian resort south of Cancun, Mexico, in January. Italian voices and Italian music sing out over the white coral sand and the palm trees. I begin to write my essay on the poetry of Pasquale Verdicchio. The setting is appropriate in this land of the lost Mayan civilization and of European colonization. Now we have the descendants of the Mayans and the Aztec learning Italian in order to be tour guides to Italian tourists who come by the thousands to visit the ruins of Mayan cities. Much like American tourists have visited Roman and Greek ruins in ancient sites around the Mediterranean, now Europeans learn that other civilizations have flourished far away in other continents. Will these change Eurocentric attitudes? Maybe the very fact that these Italians have flown eleven hours to get away from the overcrowded peninsula is a sign of changes in attitudes? Verdicchio's poems resonate in this post-colonial, post-modern environment.

From his first published poems Pasquale Verdicchio has questioned the assumptions behind the immigrant narrative. He has rejected thematics "rooted in a misguided nostalgia" (1998, 45). Coming from Naples, the capital of sentimental songs of nostalgia, he had to consciously separate himself from this tradition of heavy *malinconia*. For Verdicchio the immigrant's links with the old country are to be based on a critical view of history, a history which must also include the displaced. In many poems Verdicchio questions the role of memory and the meaning of language. Verdicchio intentionally chooses in these early poems a style that sets him apart from other Italian-Canadian poets. We will discuss this style later in the essay.

I open Verdicchio's first book of poems, *Moving Landscape* (1985), and note with irony that the fifth poem is entitled, "Mexico", and it ends with the image of a Mayan pyramid (15). This is a book that deals with the narratives of history, often the lost narratives and the silences of stone, but not the loss of meaning. Rather it is a search for new meaning. The first poem, "Red-Winged Blackbird", questions the meaning of sounds and words. What do we hear, what do we understand and what do we misunderstand? What meaning do we bring to the sound and to the words? What kind of reality does the immigrant construct from half-learned new languages and half-forgotten old ones? (11).

The next poem, "Letter", is an elegy to the dead immigrants scattered and lost. It begins with the image of the blue envelope, that is, the letter written by the far-away immigrant and captures the impulse to tell the life story: to share a life experience with family, and to link one's travels with the larger village narrative. The image of the soiled immigrant hands writing the letter epitomizes the sacrifices and suffering, the need to tell and retell the story, the lost history. The subtext in this poem is that in the official history of Italy the immigrant does not exist. For the scattered immigrants it is not only a lost history but an excluded one as well.

In addition to history there is also geography, new territories and strange place names on a page, "letters broken to mean a thousand words." Will the many travels of the immigrants add new meaning to their lives, or will their tracks all be washed away by the rains of time. The poem ends with the images of sun-bleached letters and the immigrant's sun-bleached bones turning to dust. The poet declares

> these I will use
> to make more names of places
> which may not even be (12).

It is up to the writer to give meaning to the lives and old bones of these lost and scattered immigrants. Is there an Italian diaspora? This poem gives us an image of one through scattered bones. The images of place names capture the recurrent motif in Verdicchio's verse: travel and nomadism. In the essays of this period he was exploring this problem in terms of motion and plurality. "The kinetic aspect of a work comes from writing in the present, writing as *difference*: from the origin, from itself, of its multiples, of language, announcing and losing itself" ("The Intellectual Ghetto" 53).

In other poems there is more travel across seas, over desert sands, through crowded cities and busy harbors. In "Barcelona" the aged immigrant returns to Europe as a tourist only to find that it has become culturally Americanized. We see the old culture of Europe in decay. The Spain of the conquistadors who pillaged Mexico is long gone. Even a history of great heroes cannot save a nation from its inevitable fate. It ends with an image of the famous statue of Columbus, a first immigrant, turning around in surprise at all the changes. What is the meaning of Columbus today? Is he an Italian genius, a Spanish navigator or an American icon? (23)

We turn to Verdicchio's poem, "Ancestors," and it begins to resonate with the echoes of a lost history. In many of Verdicchio's poems the author's attention to the lost meaning of words seems to subvert the narrative of Italian history, especially the lost history of immigration. In "Ancestors" he focuses on this lost history as in a dream, lost. The poet identifies the painful paradox of the Italian immigrant who must carry the burden of a great Italian culture with all its expectations, at the same time knowing that this culture has historically excluded him and continues to do so.

> Because we were the dreams
> which ancestors carved in stone
> and described in jewels
> we are now lost and confused (25).

The first stanza gives us the text for this situational contradiction. We have been taught about the great men of Italian history. It is a culture that promised greatness, but gave millions of us exile instead. The Italian immigrant is confused because even a life in exile is not his own. Instead, he seems trapped in this dream of greatness. The image has echoes of the Renaissance but also of the Fascist episode and the illusions it fostered about creating a new Roman Empire. Both periods liked great stone carvings. The second stanza continues to critique the "incomplete mosaic" of Italian culture and ends with the note of betrayal as we see the false future painted for us. The third stanza refers to the lost culture of the Etruscans, our lost ancestors. They yet remain a mystery. They probably disappeared because they we peaceful people and not warriors like the Romans. The image is of "Arms with bracelets of gold" rather than weapons of war. In the image of the arms we are reminded that both the creative artists and the destructive warriors are our ancestors.

In the fourth stanza we read that the imagination of our Italian ancestors promised much that was never fulfilled. The promise was forgotten and the dream lost. The art of the past is all that we have left: Italy as a great museum, with no room for surplus population.

This poem is one of the first that articulates the love-hate relationship of the immigrant with Italy. It rejects nostalgia and the blind filiopietism so common among Italian immigrants. The critique is all the more powerful because it is soft-spoken and un-rhetorical. It is in keeping with Verdicchio's style of using language in an unemotional manner. If we look closely we detect the anger just below the surface.

The title poem in this first collection is "Moving Landscape", an image that epitomizes the dislocation of the immigrant. Uprooted from his home village and peasant farm the immigrant will never be at ease in the new environment. In North America the landscape is unstable, always changing. Some of the changes are wrought by the immigrants themselves, who are brought to cities to rebuild and transform them. The Italians built Toronto we are told. The landscape changes back in Italy as well. First there are the abandoned villages and farms in rural areas and then the sprawl of cities and super highways. Where is the immigrant's place in this moving landscape?

> I am the only man missing
> from the landscape
> of a ready-made history (41).

When reading these opening lines what "ready-made history" comes to mind? We may think that it is the majority history of North America, a narrative dominated by the English and the French with a few token native chiefs and Spanish generals. The Italian immigrant is certainly absent from this official history. But the "ready-made history" is also that of Italy, a history of great artists and heroes. A master narrative that has not included the millions of departing emigrants. By definition they "subtract everything / nothing must be left over." The emigrant is missing from the Italian landscape and is only evident if you look for his absence.

The culture of the immigrant is that of absences. The immigrants "function as an absence" in both the home landscape and the new one. The second stanza begins with the image of a "city built of many departures." This city could be any city like Naples or it could be Italy itself. The immigrants who left contributed to the future possibilities of Italy as much as those who remained behind. There is an old Italian saying which is the reverse of this idea, "Parte anche qui resta." It literally means that those who remain also leave, and refers to the lasting effects of family break-up, the loss of a father, a son or a brother (Pitto). The rapid departure of hundreds of thousands of emigrants in the decades after WWII changed the face of Italy and the dynamics in rural farms, villages and city businesses. The immediate benefits were that there were fewer demands on the limited social resources and on the impoverished economy. This contributed directly to Italy's economic recovery in the 1960s and 1970s. In the third stanza there is the metamorphosis enacted on the immigrant body by others. Displacement results in physical change, but it also causes a change in identity over which the immigrant has no control. He finds himself separated from the past with words. The words are English and do put distance between the speaker and his Italian origins. The transformation is enacted from the outside and makes him a different person. Is this new language a mask you wear? The deeper reality, the Italian one, is now hiding. The speaker observes that

There is no language without deceit.
A Grammar of bodies and images
grown out of false form. (42)

As long as the speaker uses words he must continue to pretend, to accept the transformation. The only escape possible is through silence. Years pass and only at night, in the black on black, can the speaker begin to recover lost memories of this past. He asks if there is any thing that remains of him in the old land, a lost sound perhaps. He can only imagine a return to the old shore. Is it an illusion, or only a dream?

The poem continues with images of his dying mother and lost memory. It is a very slow and painful death as we try to recover memory and construct poems. Besides the dead mother there is the dead language and dead words. The black of burning pages turning to night produces more poems to welcome death. Does writing poetry keep death at bay?

The immigrant sees destiny in following the horizon, travelling under different skies. He asks questions about destiny, "caught between ambiguity of surfaces" (45). We are caught for a short time, our lives, between two identities and two languages. The memories of stone and fire end with the striking image of "tongue-tied ruins."

"Moving Landscape" is Verdicchio's major poem of this period and illustrates his main literary preoccupations: the rejection of nostalgia, the questioning of a national history which excludes a major part of the population and its exodus. We also note the absence of any personal references or any suggestion of a confessional mode. There is a feeling of alienation in these verses reflected in the suppression of the personal. Is this alienation also mirrored in the use of the fragmented language in parts of the poems?

The chapbook that follows, *Moving Landscape,* is called appropriately, *Ipsissima Verba* (1986), and begins with images of the moving landscape, fragments of memory and lost voices. In the different poems Verdicchio examines the problems of language and of home. In the poem, "This House, That House," he examines the different types of home: the home of distance, the home of division, the home away from home, and the home constructed. Is the perpetual wanderer, the immigrant dreaming of home? The next book is called, *Nomadic Trajectory* (1990) and continues the pattern of moving across landscapes and across borders, forever. In another chapbook, *A Critical Geography,* (1989) Verdicchio develops similar travels in space and time. Some Italian locations are suggested with references to fig tree, Ionian Sea, olive tree, rosary and saints.

Style

At the conference of Italian-Canadian writers in Vancouver in 1986 Pasquale Verdicchio presented a paper which outlined his poetic style as distinct from that of most other Italian-Canadian poets. In "The Failure of Memory in the Language Re-Membering of Italian-Canadian Poets," Verdicchio discusses the problems of languages, of choosing to work in one of Canada's official languages while the Italian language acts as interference with the memories of Italian culture. He points to the use of Italian words and phrases within poems written in English or French as a way of reclaiming a language and a culture that have become distant. This is a common stylistic practice among many Italian-Canadian writers, but one that Verdicchio rejects as "contradictory and self-defeating" (118). He explains that this style underscores cultural and social alienation since the Italian words are isolated among English or French words. To Verdicchio the process of remembering, of piecing together the fragments of a culture, is undermined since it expresses difference with itself. He sees the mere act of trying to possess Italian at a distance as self-deceptive.

> When the instinctual search takes place in the language of poetry it turns away from English or French to find emptiness. And though the mother-language makes itself felt, it is distant, out of reach. The need for its expression manifests itself through an act of will, the voluntary, though irrational, use of one Italian word or another. (119)

In rejecting this model of language retrieval through poetry Verdicchio set himself apart from many of his Italian-Canadian contemporaries. To some his poetry seemed less Italian since it used only English diction and often an abstract English. The irony of this position is that Verdicchio in his profession teaches Italian at the university level. Did he feel less distant from the mother language than his contemporaries who had to work completely in English and may have felt a greater loss of their original language? In his comments of their style he repeatedly points out that they are trying to consciously recover the lost culture through the re-acquisition of the half-forgotten language.

In his diction Verdicchio does not include any Italian words, phrases or even names. Only in the odd title like "Pasqua" is there any hint of an Italian reference. While we often get the personal point of view of the speaker, there are no personal references from the poet himself. There are no references to family members or family events in Canada or in Italy. There are no grandparents. While there are powerful images and striking metaphors there is not emotional language in this verse: no mamma, romantic lover, children, religion or anger. Much ethnic minority writing has the autobiographical story just beneath the surface of the poem or narrative. For Verdicchio any biographical element has been submerged. It is as if he does not trust the language of personal emotion. And maybe this reflects the experience of dislocation and of having to acquire a strange language which does not have an emotional register for the newcomer.

Where are the Italian aspects of Verdicchio's poetry? These are not as obvious as in other Italian-Canadian writers. The subject of Italian immigration is the pervasive one in these early poems. "Moving

Landscape" cannot be understood outside of this context of physical displacement and of deterritorialization of language. There is the repeated critique of Italian history and modern society. At times this critique is a subtext as in "Letter." The abstract language and calm tone apparently hide the emotional force behind the poems, and the anger is there as well.

The poems do not indulge in any overt immigrant nostalgia because there is so much of it in Italian popular culture and music. His native Naples is famous for its sentimental songs such as, "O Sole Mio," and "Te Vojo Bene Assai." Verdicchio is consciously reacting to this and as such is also part of the historical discourse (Bakhtin). He focuses on the geographical displacement which is the major change in any immigration. Verdicchio's treatment of the nomadic recurs in many poems and several of his collections. And we must recognize that this motif of travel reflects his own life migrations from Naples to Vancouver to Edmonton and then to San Diego, California, with many long stays back in Italy.

Pasquale Verdicchio's preoccupation with language and meaning is part of the subject of geographical displacement. Only someone who must deal with the reality of two or more languages, especially as an immigrant, would develop such a sense of the ambiguity of words and meanings. In many of these early poems a reader is struck by the sparse use of words. This minimalist style puts more weight and meaning on each word, but it also brings out the ambiguity of words. These word patterns can have several meanings, or can just be beautiful word patterns. Any reader cannot help but feel that the fragmentary style in several of these poems reflects the loss of meaning for words and for language. We will have to explore the development of this process in Verdicchio's latter poetry and essays and see if we must revise our impressions of these early poems. With his poetry and his literary essays Pasquale Verdicchio is one of the Italian-Canadian authors who has inspired me to publish books such as *Echo: Essay on Other Literatures.*

Works Cited

Bakhtin, M.M. *The Dialogic Imagination.* Austin: University of Texas Press, 1981.

Pitto, Cesare. *Al di là dell'emigrazione.* Spezzano Albanese: Ionica Editrice, 1988.

Pivato, Joseph. *Echo: Essays on Other Literatures.* Toronto: Guernica Editions, 2003.

Verdicchio, Pasquale. *Moving Landscape.* Montreal: Guernica Editions, 1985.

_____. *Ipsissima Verba.* La Jolla, Ca.: Parentheses Writing Series, 1986.

_____. *A Critical Geography.* La Jolla, Ca.: Parentheses Writing Series, 1989.

_____. *Nomadic Trajectory.* Montreal: Guernica Editions, 1990.

_____. "The Failure of Memory in the Language Re-Membering of Italian-Canadian Poets." *Writers in Transition.* eds. C.D.

Minni & Anna Foschi Ciampolini. Montreal: Guernica Editions, 1990.

_____. "L'Italia in Bocca." *Vice Versa*, 36 (Mars, 1992), 21-23.

_____. "Italian Canadian cultural politics: the contradictions of representation." *Altreitalie*, 17 (gennaio-giugno, 1998), 42-47.

_____. "Introduction," Antonio Gramsci. *The Southern Question.* West Lafayette: Bordighera, Inc., 1995

ANNA ZAMPIERI PAN AND
PASQUALE VERDICCHIO

INTERVIEW: NEW CULTURAL PATHS

ANNA ZAMPIERI PAN: You left Naples as an adolescent. Decades later, having studied and with mostly a North American cultural baggage, what significance do you assign memory and how do you perceive of your identity?

PASQUALE VERDICCHIO: This is, of course, always a difficult question. Off-the-cuff I would say that my identity is Italian, but identity is a very complex thing to define precisely. I would prefer maybe something like "citizen of the world", but this is a facile and banal answer. What I will say, however, is that, after so many years in San Diego, I still cannot full identify with the place in which I live. Not only the city, but the nation, the very concept of nation in the U.S.A., the nationalist, ideological sense what citizenship, belonging, assimilation, and adaptation might mean, I find difficult south of the border.

I have lived longer in the U.S.A. than in Italy or in Canada. Strangely enough, I came to identify myself more as a Canadian once I moved to the U.S.A. As for a sense of uninterrupted identification, more fluid, and as cultural and social affinity I identify myself as Italian. This was complicated somewhat by my unexpected and temporary loss of my Italian citizenship in 1998, right at the moment in which I was moving back to live in Italy for two years. Having gone to renew my passport at the Italian Consulate in Los Angeles, I suddenly found myself to be an *extra-comunitario*, a non-member of the EU Community. For reasons that I find completely ludicrous, a policy toward some Italians living abroad — a purely bureaucratic reason — has made it possible to take away our citizenship. I am speaking in the plural because I know others who are in the same situation; my case is not unique. It is a policy that needs reviewing and correction, especially in light of the thousands of citizenships that were approved to two and three generations of Italian descendants born abroad, some of whom had never set foot in Italy.

Memory. I don't know if memory reigns absolute in my relationship with Italy, because I have lived there for long periods over the years, periods that go from months to years. I also return regularly, sometimes once or twice a year. I am not saying that I do not feel an "outsider", but those of us who live abroad can probably only aspire to that as an identity. We are outside of every situation, always living somewhere between events, situations, occurrences, looking in more directions at any single moment. We are bound to always living abroad, internally abroad, a suitcase full of *abroadness,* which we carry with us back and forth. Our culture will never be pure, single, easily identifiable. That's why I believe that our culture and our identity represent the future: it will be our children's culture and the culture of future societies. Canada, or at least the Vancouver that I see today, is very close to that sort of culture. This city today is very different from the Vancouver that we came to decades ago. I prefer this Vancouver for many reasons, even though it has strayed too close to, and slipped almost without noticing it, materialism and consumerism, dangers that intellectuals like Pier Paolo Pasolini identified clearly.

AZP: Living between Canada, the U.S.A., and Italy, and with the curiosity and possibility of exploring other parts of the world, would it be appropriate to refer to you as a nomad?

PV: I've always had an affinity for that image and, yes, I see myself in it to some extent. In fact, one of my poetry collections is entitled *Nomadic Trajectory* (Guernica Editions). It's important to remember though that the nomad does not move chaotically without a goal or objective in the landscape. The image of the nomad that I value is that of the traveler who moves between existing sites, yet ones that are in constant transformation. The nomad is also one who reads the landscape in every single detail, as traces of signs that are useful to survival. Nomadism is a culture of adoption and adaptation. Travel takes place between sites, and the intervals along the longer path are of utmost importance. Constantine Cavafy's poem *Ithaca* is often quoted as an illustration of this notion: what is important is not arriving in Ithaca, but the voyage toward the city. My travels are often between known points of departure and arrival: San Diego, the desert east of San Diego, Vancouver, Savary Island, Napoli, Lanciano, Bologna. Familiar places to which I return over and over, places that are known to me that nevertheless, time after time, year after year, reveal and offer new dimensions of themselves that generate new experiences. If they did not, I would most likely not return to them.

AZP: What are your reference points?

PV: Obviously one's acquaintances, those one meets, and the friendships that might develop, are the first reference points. On the other hand, I am not so certain as to what my reference points might be, or even if I have any. Most of my traveling has been solitary, without family, with long periods of solitude. It is a physical traveling toward other places that expresses itself internally, without reference points.

AZP: What role does family play for you?

PV: I may seem to be full of contradictions, because for me the family is of utmost importance. It was very important for us to have relatives in Vancouver when we arrived; arriving with the certainty of knowing someone made it for a softer landing in a completely foreign place and culture. Our experience in Vancouver would likely have been more difficult without that support group. Today, even though I may not feel completely at home in California, I feel rooted in and with my family. Our children were born in San Diego; they are American, Canadian, and European citizens.

My mother, brothers, and other relatives define Vancouver as a reference point. I can't say whether someday these places will retain their importance or not. I do feel a sense of coming home when we travel to British Columbia. As one ages it will be important to define a comfortable place in which to settle more permanently. And then, of course, there is community, another element that is important for me. Given my distance from Vancouver, I haven't been active in the Italian community as much as I would have hoped to be. In fact, my participation in the writing community and in the foundation of the Association of Italian Canadian Writers began shortly before I moved to the U.S.A. Arriving in San Diego, I found an Italian community that was full of potential and cultural possibilities. I worked hard to organize meetings, the first community-based conference, film screenings, gathering of history and historical artifacts. Those projects slowly seem to have reached a point where some forces in the community found the intervention of an outsider a threat, which led me to shutting down a small archive and cultural center that I had opened with a friend, Robert Marino. I am happy to say, however, that those initiatives that we began and put forward had their impact and may have moved things in directions that may not have manifested otherwise.

I also had an adopted community in Lanciano, Abruzzo, where the possibility of creating a North America/Italia bridge existed, but was again negated by local opposition by some players in the community. The distrust of outsiders seems to be part of our DNA, and often results in undermining our own progress in order to prevent others from achieving some amount of success. Nevertheless, when the more immediate ties of family are missing, community building and participation are very important. That is where cultural exploration and production of new paths begin. In order to achieve some functionality, we also need to expand on our understanding of *accoglienza* (welcoming), a term that must carry its validity across the spectrum of backgrounds and cultures that those newly arrived to our shores (in Canada, the U.S.A., or Italy) bring to meet our own.

There are various ways of attracting people to what Italian culture has to offer. Given the recent World Cup success, I think that enrollments in Italian language and culture courses will see an increase. Italian culture is one *of* and *from* community: it is based on the social, on showing and show on living and sharing, even when one is in apparent solitude.

AZP: How much *italianità* can there be in Italians living abroad, often living among other cultures and ethnicities? Is there a process of hybridism that slowly begins to take place?

PV: This is something that really does not concern me at all. There has always been hybridization. The most dangerous and detrimental thing that can affect a community or a nation is to consider itself "pure". And Italians, in particular, have never been anything but a hybrid population. Just considering the geographical position of the peninsula should be enough to put any notion of ethnic purity to bed. Why waste so much energy, cause so much suffering for some idealized fictions that we sustain with I.D. cards and passports? I am not saying that we should abolish all borders; we should merely recognize who we all are: human beings, without any pretense of superior or inferior bloodlines without ethnicity or a pure race. Culture is what happens when people meet.

I don't believe in *italianità* as a concept expressive of our culture. It is a term too closely tied to the dictates of fascism. Even if we were to re-propose it today as a way to describe a global culture related to Italy, in my opinion we could do better. I would prefer something like *italicità* (which finds one of its strongest advocates in the writer Antonio D'Alfonso), as a gesture toward a culture that has some of its roots on Italic territory and subsequently spread out to other geographic areas, mostly through emigration. *Italicità* is also meant to express expatriation as a response to certain conditions that are distant from the colonial intentionality that the term *italianità* has trouble shedding. Historically, emigration resulted in an Italic cultural evolution produced abroad among Italy's emigrated population and its descendants. Whether one speaks Italian or not, as descendants and participants of this Italic evolution, we are expressions of a transformed Italian culture. There may possibly be very little *italianità* that Italians in Italy might recognize in those who live abroad. Nevertheless, we are connected by the fact of descendants, however minimal and tenuous that fact may be.

AZP: As an artist and man of culture, how do you view the relationship between culture and politics? What are the points of their encounter or contrast? What do you think of the right to vote given to Italians abroad?

PV: Not as an artist or man of culture, but as a person who lives among others, the relationship between culture and politics is, in my view, undeniable. It's impossible to make culture in a void. Culture happens when we encounter each other; that encounter is political, because it implies a certain way to relate to each other that will decide its success or failure.

I don't really understand authors and artists who declare themselves to be apolitical. How can one speak, write, paint, make film, without acknowledging that each act, sign, word or shout carries with it a history of usage and interpretation? How can one negate the interpretation of these same things on the part of others who consume those cultural products? One can certainly say not to be politicized in the making of art, but the materials themselves don't really leave us any option. The points of encounter and contrast are many. The ones that I have most recently encountered in my activities have to do with a series of films that I presented for the Italian community of San Diego. Some individuals reacted very strongly, politically, as if films represented my own political opinion. That's fine, up to a certain point; I don't mind this sort of encounter at all. However, it so happens that sometimes these moments have been taken as a platform from which to launch into political rhetoric with a very direct target, in order to manipulate political elections, which takes me to another part of your question, regarding extending the vote in Italian elections to Italians abroad.

I am of the opinion that extending the vote to Italians abroad does not necessarily make sense. Most Italians abroad know little of Italian politics and do not necessarily follow its ups and downs. I am talking mostly about the great number of individuals who have more recently acquired their citizenship. These are individuals whose interest is mostly related to acquiring citizenship as a form of nostalgia, which was illustrated quite well by their low turnout to vote in the last referendum. In order to make for a more efficacious and realistic representation of Italians abroad, Italian Consulates and Cultural Institutes would have to become much more involved and active within Italian American communities. After more than thirty years of teaching at the University of California, San Diego, I can tell you that San Diego and its universities are practically non-existent as far as the Consulate and Cultural Institute are concerned. Both Italian institutions are located in Los Angeles.

AZP: Even though you live and work in San Diego, you are frequently in Vancouver, your first place of arrival in North America, your family's place of residence, and where your secondary and post-secondary education took place. You left here while quite young. Would you come back to live here, perhaps work?

PV: Yes, I would gladly come back. As I've said, even after such a long residence there, I still feel San Diego to be a place of passage. I may eventually feel Californian whenever I leave, but for now Vancouver is my city. My wife is from British Columbia; both our families reside in Vancouver. We come back a number of times a year. In the summer we come back for a month or two; we go to Savary Island, where we own a small house. For a Neapolitan *guaglione*, I find myself quite at home in the forests of B.C. Not having had the opportunity of finding an academic position in Canada early on, after a while the decision to remain in San Diego became a natural outcome, as both my wife and I have set deeper roots in our work-places.

AZP: What is the fundamental message that you are passing on to your students and your children?

PV: I would simply cite a few verses by Gary Snyder. As time move on, as the challenges of our relationship to each other and the earth require more and more attention, these verses take on a more impactful meaning. I read this to my students at the end of some of my classes. They express some of my own aspirations:

> To climb these coming crests
> one word to you, to
> you and your children:
>
> stay together
> learn the flowers
> go light.
> *(For the children)*

Note

Previously published in *Personaggi & Persone*, Vol. 1, pp. 159-165, and in *People, Places, Passages: An Anthology of Canadian Writing*, pp. 423-429, Montreal: Longbridge Book, 2018. This version has been slightly altered to account for some more recent developments.

DIEGO BASTIANUTTI

LETTER TO PASQUALE

It doesn't matter who our father was;
what matters is who we remember he was.

READING YOUR DIARY "Father" and the sequence of dreams as a form of closure following your father's death brought to mind a number of parallels you and I share. You see, like you I was born in Via Belvedere, you in Napoli, and I in Fiume, some fifteen years earlier. We both immigrated to North America for different reasons and in different circumstances. Both of us professed our Italian culture in university, but while I started in the U.S.A. and ended in Canada, you did just the reverse. Your father, like mine, is buried in the land in which he planted new roots. Like you, but for different motives, I feel like an intruder in my native city. Finally, as you I had a dream about my own father some forty years ago, in my case it was a premonitory dream.

It happened in Venice where I was teaching a course. One night, I had the most bizarre dream: I was climbing toward a small thatched-roof cottage perched on top of a knoll. I had no idea what it was, but something compelled me to knock on its door.

After no one answered my repeated calls, and I was about to turn away, when I reached inside my coat pocket and felt something heavy. I pulled out a large antique key. I remembered finding it by chance in the hollow of a tree trunk and had decided to keep it. I felt as if this was a message of sort: a mysterious house, a locked door, and an equally mysterious ancient key. I went up to the door again, inserted the key and turned it clockwise three times. Nothing, the door remained closed. I decided to turn the key counterclockwise and suddenly some pins clicked and the door swung open. Apparently I was in a world operating in reverse. I stepped into what appeared to be a one-room cottage permeated with the fragrance of apples, though I could not see any in the room. As I looked down, I realized I was walking on a floor made of crystal and I could see snowflakes falling up toward me from below. In my dream, that seemed normal. As in your dream, it seemed I was living a world in reverse, yet as you, I accepted this as though it had "been going on for millennia." Someone knocking at the door then distracted me. I went to open it and there, standing before me, was my father in his suit, smiling as he stepped inside the cottage. A few months later, I was called to his bedside. He had terminal cancer.

Following my father's death, I went through the same process as you. My father was gone, and gone with him were my strongest and deepest roots. Gone in a breath. One moment I was there with him, holding his hand and a second later he went quiet, his hand growing cold in mine. Hours later, I could still hear the echo of his voice.

Losing my father, my *papà*, was to realize that I would never again say the word *papà* to him. "When your father dies," say the Russians, "he takes your childhood with him." I was the one on the front line, no longer shielded by the generation that had preceded me. I suddenly felt abandoned, naked. I was the one charged with building on my father's moral and cultural legacy. I wondered if I could carry it off with my children as well as he had with me.

At first, it was a rough struggle in which my mood went from resentment for his loss to serenity in recalling the peaceful smile on my father's face when he gently asked to let him go. It was in these contrasting moments that my memories of him slowly rose to mind, much like stones rise to the surface in springtime.

Then, as time passed, the process of remembering my father in greater detail became similar to the slow developing of a negative, watching the gradual emergence of shadows and contrasts that placed in sharper relief the final image. I remember the effect my father's wedding ring had on me. The sight of it, now on my own hand, brought more recollections to the surface, "events" of which I had had no conscious memory until then. The small details of his life, the ones I hardly noticed when he was alive, grew into revelations. I was finally able to connect small insignificant events into a character-revealing pattern. I marveled at the hidden part of his life I was discovering.

As I watched my mother during the weeks following my father's passing, I saw her in a different light. I realized what he had meant to her, how together they had faced the challenges of the war and post-war period, the emigration with two teenage children to a new country, without any citizenship papers. As I say in verses dedicated to my father:

> A war left you orphan of a childhood
> with grownup cares, orphaned of the love
> and affection you sought all your life
>
> Yet in so many crucial moments of our life
> you found the dignity and the strength
> to pilot us safely across wars and oceans
> hand in hand with mamma (Lost in Transit, 2019).

I saw the void she felt not having his strength at her side. I also understood the great influence she had exercised over her husband, my father. I admired the life they had built together for us with the cards life had dealt them, and suddenly I felt a love, pride, and respect for them I had never felt before to such a degree. I just regretted not having spent more time with him, instead of desperately and perhaps selfishly searching for ways to save him.

I felt guilty that only after he was gone I began to really know and understand my father better. I began to notice in many small ways how much I was like him. I became something of an archeologist of my own self through the memories of my father. To use your words, "at times it felt as if I had found myself after being missing for years" (75).

As for you, Pasquale, keeping vigil with my father on his last journey had turned into a "visit that required an accounting of all our lives" (68). It was chilling at first but, as the persona of my father filled out to become much more than I had ever imagined, I rejoiced in the discovery. In his death I saw the essence of his life, a man's life. This was for me the last chance to understand myself through my father. It was my father's last gift to me.

This is what your sensitive diary offered me, it conjured up my own painful process of self-discovery so many years ago.

Memory ties together events scattered across our space-time continuum which constitutes us. We exist in time. So to understand ourselves means reflecting on time and, as Carlo Rovelli says, reflecting on time means reflecting about ourselves. Time exists only in the present, in our mind, in the form of memory and anticipation. This is the source of our identity.

We are our memory, our nostalgia, our yearning for a possible-impossible future, and thanks to this marvelous gift, we are able to laugh, cry, and taste with unchanged freshness the events of our "past" with equal joy in the limited span of time life gives each of us.

In the diary you reveal a profound understanding of life through a cultured and sensitive soul, and the rare ability to see the true meaning of events while they are taking place. You are desperately clinging to the threads which linked you to your father. The life-giving or life-preserving function of such threads is a well-known mythological motif. The Fates spin the thread of man's life, and Theseus finds his way out of the Minoan Labyrinth thanks to Ariadne's thread.

You use photography the way Helen of Troy uses weaving as a way of fulfilling her need to overcome death by producing an artifact which will survive her and "tell her story", her *kleos*, to all future generations. Unlike Andromache who, upon receiving news of Hector's death, enters into a state of complete and irretrievable loss of identity, you realize that the memory of your father will keep him alive and ensure your own identity in the evolving reality.

The reality of our space-time is a fabric resulting from the ceaseless interaction of individual experiences — all made up of memories — a spider web with a finite number of distinct threads. We exist when we interact with each other or with our own memories. The black hole of time swallows up our past, which we thwart by recounting and reliving our memories.

If we do have a *soul*, it must be the sum total of encounters in which humans relate with one another in a way that reaches profoundly into the very essence of our individual, cultural and historical collective self. Marvin Minsky thinks that *soul* is the word we use for each person's idea of what they are and why. The neologism *souling* is what researches claim emerges from the interaction between our bodies and our environment. What Ortega y Gasset would say in defining the "I": *Yo soy yo y mis circumstancias* (I am I plus my circumstances).

What we think and what we physically feel and what we emotionally feel are all related. It is impossible to draw hard boundaries between them. This is what you, Pasquale, deal with when you observe your father's shriveling body and when you touch with loving tenderness his gnarled hands:

> I spread moisturizing lotion on them, since his skin has gotten even drier. The patterns on his knuckles and finger joints have worn smooth and flat. Smooth skin with no identifying marks of any sort, this is the legacy of hard work. I run my hands over them to feel the smoothness that has itself become an identifying absence (78).

In *The Accidental Universe* Alan Lightman tells us that "science has vastly expanded the scale of our cosmos, but our emotional reality is still limited by what we can touch with our own bodies in the time span of our lives." He reminds us that we are not observers looking in from the outside. We too are on the inside. As the recently departed Toni Morrison said, "I dream a dream that dreams back at me." In the end, she realizes that, "I am all the things I have ever loved." A concept you confirm through the verses of Gianni Celati:

Tutto ciò che ti attraversa non sei tu,
eppure tu sei solo questo.

[We are not what passes through us,
and yet that is all we are.]

You, the observer, cannot be separated from your father the observed:

I watch you
Watch me
Watch the world (30)

You watch as your father in the hospital bed "floats there, lighter than his heavy life", and dives deep into his past to revisit places of his life in another world in another time but "holding out his hand as if to ask me to reel him back into the room where it all started" (71). I recall how my own father, on the contrary, kept begging not to be pulled back from where he was going alone ever deeper, from what he would later describe as a place of peace and serenity.

[65]

Accompanying your father in his last journey meant also bridging Italy and Canada, two different cultures and the life experience of two overlapping generations into one. It was the inner and the outer calling out to fuse as one in you.

> The years, after all, have a kind of emptiness when we spend too many of them on a foreign shore. We defer the reality of life, in such cases, until a future moment, when we shall again breathe our native air; but by and by, there are no future moments; or, if we do return, we find that the native air has lost its invigorating quality, and that life has shifted its reality to the spot where we have deemed ourselves only temporary residents. Thus, between two countries, we have none at all, or only that little space of either in which we finally lay down our discontented bones (Nathaniel Hawthorne, "Black Sun...").

Hawthorne addresses the very question faced by you and so many other emigrants. Both you and your father have memories of two different worlds: the Italy you left and the Canada where your family created a new life. But while everyone is always an exile from his past, those like us with a double set of cultures will often feel like "outlanders" or, as I define myself, an "antevasin": an in-betweener, a border-dweller who lives in sight of two worlds, two cultures, two quite different mindsets, and a multiplicity of memories and emotions that have to be reconciled in an attempt to redefine his identity. Nomadism, exile, distances "marked by maps / and stained envelopes":

> There will be no survivors
> In the war of identity
> We will be the only one
> To recognize ourselves
> To keep our reciprocal memory
> Of distance alive
> To witness other time
> Other habits other ancestries
>
> What remain of exile
> If not our absence
> And our denial (53).

In the end you and I must deal with all that we inherit from our fathers, be it negative or positive. Neither can be denied nor eradicated, they are part of us, a manifestation that defines our identity. Your voyage inward like your father's "must be so deep and confusing that the return to the surface is always in question" (70).

Even though for years you have been living and teaching in San Diego, the city

> remains foreign and unsettling. My mind is always not here. My body feels alone. My emotions, without a place to root, have settled on the surface of my skin (66).

There are aspects of ourselves which we can find only by re-visiting the place we left, because it means returning to that part of ourselves we have sacrificed when we emigrated. Yet, even going back often does not resolve anything, as you are forced to admit when you return to your beloved Napoli:

I cannot read or experience anything here without considering it in light of our absence of decades. How does culture exist in the altered perspective created by the non-resident portion of the population it was meant to express? (66)

In much the same way neither can you "read or experience anything" in San Diego or in Vancouver without considering it in light of your early formative years in Napoli. I too went through the same process many years ago as I recorded in many of my poems:

Restare non posso più inchiodato / al perno del bisogno fatto ragione / sconfitto devo tornare / alla slabbrata costa dei miei morti / sconfitto dalla nostalgia / di una tenace primavera perduta.

[I can no longer stay nailed / to the post of need / turned purpose / I must return defeated / to my fathers' jagged shores / defeated by the nostalgia / for a long-lost yet / unforgotten spring.]

and later:

Voglio vedere / se quell'antica alchimia / fra la linfa e la mia terra / nutrirsi può non solo / di parola ricordata / di gesto nel sangue ripetuto,/ eco di essenza che in rimandi / da un passato ormai remoto / man mano si sbiadisce /

[I want to see / if that ancient alchemy / between my lymph and my land / can cease to suckle solely / on words recalled / on mien repeated in the blood / echoes of an essence that / in a replicated past now quite remote / day by day grows more faint]

. . . in esilio, qua / dove la luce è schiacciata / in vertigine orizzontale fra cielo e terra / qua dove la vita si inserisce / fra minima eredità di orecchie / e ancora meno memoria di bocca.

[… here, in exile, / where light is crushed in level vertigo / between earth and sky / here where life happens / between trivial heredity of ears / and even less memory of mouth.]

But in the end, I too reach a synthesis and make a choice:

Ora, rientrato in questa terra / di mia libera scelta, / con la compagna per mano / sereno lascio scivolare dall'altra / quell misero pugno di terra / ormai faccio parte del futuro / per quel che sono: / un meticcio.

[Now, having returned to this land / of my own free will, / hand in hand with my love happily I let run through my fingers / the handful of that other soil / I'm part of the future / because of what I am: a *mestizo*

(Per un pugno di terra / For a Fistful of Soil, 2006).

And so we begin a dialogue between what we can define as "historical truth" and "narrative truth", and it will include both our personal memories as well as those of others we have made our own. Our memory is dialogical, because it is generated not only by our direct experience but also by a continuous exchange with others. The only truth is the narrative truth, the stories we tell others and ourselves, the stories we continually polish. Our sense of identity is closely tied to our memory, both individual and collective. To understand ourselves we need to go back to the beginning of our lives, analyze the influences that have shaped us, the people that have been important to us. This is the journey you, Pasquale, undertook as you kept vigil.

What often results is that people that have faced some form of *displacement* have gone through an identity crisis involving a sort of negotiation between their *present self* and *the other*, especially when these are in conflict. The result is a transitional identity, a hybrid identity which may or may not be resolved eventually. When dealing with so-called "strong" cultures, we might end up with interior *parallel universes*. Only those who are able to create bridges to connect these two universes will be able to navigate successfully in both societies.

We are implicitly asking here at what point does an immigrant cease to be one. Is it when he feels more at home in the adopted country? Or is it also when the adopting country stops seeing him/her as an immigrant? Because in the end that is what is most important: the immigrant has done all he could to integrate in the host country, but all that is for naught unless that society goes the extra step to assimilate him. Something you recognize when you sum up both yours and your father's lives:

> Odd how at the end it's like at the beginning, how the sum of our long residence in this country is still drawn to signify foreignness (75).

What is the rapport between identity and territory? Does the immigrant develop some sort of *ethnoscape* of his constant shifting between two worlds, or it is better to use the term *mindscape* to define the way the immigrant finally resolves the conflict of two worlds and two different cultures, each essential in defining his identity. This is, indeed, the question you pose in the end:

> Does the image of a person change after emigration? … Is one's bodily difference a result of age or distance from one's former self, one's other self, a self more recognizable and familiar. How does one change when migrated away from one's self? (83)

I fully agree with you as I express in the poem "Lost in Transit":

> I am the world in which I breathe
> displaced from my ancestral land
> as much as from myself
>
> Yet even now my very own past
> has become a foreign land to me

where what I see and hear and feel
is no longer mine
and as the years grow heavy
the more I feel as if I'm treading
a land twice foreign
Time has displaced me
as much as distance so long ago
all has become once more so alien

("Lost in Transit", 2019).

Ultimately, it is a question of negotiating one's place in this world rather than knowing one's place. It involves recognizing Pavese's ultimate truth, the impossible *nostos* or return home.

In the end, through a profoundly evocative sequence of dreams, you achieve the goal of finding yourself, because to *be* yourself you must *have* yourself, possess yourself and, if necessary, take back the story of your life. You have to "repeat" yourself, recall all dramatic events in your life, maintain a continuous interior monologue in order to retain and preserve your identity, your true inner *self*. In a wonderful dream image you are able to recognize and accept your inner self humming the same tune as the child you embraces: the union of the two parallel universes.

I notice a woman coming toward me. Can't quite make out who it might be. She is carrying a child of one or two . . . As I reach them, the child reaches out and embraces me, placing his head against mine. And we stand there, forehead to forehead, the child embracing me as it hums a tune, I too begin to hum this tune and a wonderfully light and happy feeling comes over me and I smile and smile and smile. I wake up happy and smiling.

You have traced the geography of your being. Now you are whole.

CARMELO MILITANO

THE MIND, THE BODY, LANGUAGE, AND IMAGE

PASQUALE VERDICCHIO WEARS a variety of hats: poet, university teacher, translator, essayist, and critic. In each role he is engaged in the business of talking about culture, writing, Italian cinema, literature, and history. His interest includes an on-going examination of where Italian culture (the mother country) intersects with the Italian diaspora or immigration experience.

His poetry collection, *This Nothing's Place*, sits between two different publications: *Duologue* (1998), a recorded artistic dialogue between Pasquale Verdicchio and writer Antonio D'Alfonso, and his scholarly work *Looters, Photographers, and Thieves* (2011), a study of nineteenth- and twentieth-century Italian photographic culture. *This Nothing's Place* is an extension of Verdicchio's interest in place and identity and on how these are created and interact with one another. What is created can be placed in the wider context of how cultural images and writings serve (or don't serve) larger social and political interests.

These poems grapple with the issues of locating place, the body, the self, the interaction of photographic images, and memory, and Verdicchio achieves this in a quieter and less explicit manner as compared to his oral discussion and his written expository academic prose. As one can expect, Verdicchio is more personal in his poetry.

The first poem "M" illustrates this point as it gathers up a series of small, almost throw away incidents, to move us toward a reckoning about the larger theme of connection. It begins with the left over (abandoned?), the barely noticeable things inside an empty classroom. "May Light", "a coloured head-band", a shy smile, and a "self-conscious hand" are examples of the small, the unadorned, and the casual, evoking solitary stillness. The silence of a classroom once alive with students: the empty, muted stillness inside the empty classroom is poignant with the intimate objects left behind or remembered (the head-band and the self-conscious smile). These extensions reflect the silence the poet recognizes and is part of M's body.

> The silence of your body
> accompanies me
> across the landscape
> of comings and goings.

The silence connects the narrator to M, "opens" the poet, and guides him to M. In fact, silence has transformed and exposed the poet, or at the very least has led to the unmasking of self, now a kind of love. His heart now revealed, silence is the cause of the poet's connection to M: the silence between two lovers, un-expectedly discovering intimacy.

If the self in this poem is able to locate itself in re-lation to the silence found in the body of the other, the poet in "This House" seeks to locate the self and body and to discuss how language works or fails in relation to self and body. The poem asserts that "the slight of the everyday / and the nothing that is residence / then the order of the word / would coincide with hidden names." Words, in other words, crack open the world, reveal the hidden spaces inside or outside "the edge of . . . inhabitation". In this poem, unlike in "M", we are "on the lawn of mouth to mouth" where in the declin-ing light ("waning light"), the tip-of-the-tongue place where one can just about identify and locate ourselves in relation to the place where language and self might intersect. Words "spin" and reveal the everyday living, the mouth-to-mouth of common speech. Language discloses and centers the self in relation to place. It is a strange heroic everyday act, this common use of lan-guage against "the nothing that is residence" or, if you like, the existential impermanence of place and life it-self. All is provisional. "If this house were to stand" and "if we were to stand / for all that distance / has come to mean / for the slight of the everyday" suggest a poet who sees language as the only possibility to an-chor existence as well as being the vehicle by which we express and construct the proverbial sand castle on the beach. It is, finally, how knowledge, experience, and language interact to mark and construct the world.

In the last section of this collection Verdicchio writes a series of prose poems on the themes of place, self, the dissonance of immigration, death and loss, the slow dissolve of the body, and in particular the poet's father. The prose ruminations are grouped under the general rubric "Father". Under this rubric are four sections: "First Death", "Final Death", "Dreams After Death", and "Postscript". Each section is a rumination on the past: the poet's father and the poet himself struggling to understand and place into some kind of perspective his father's life and work in contrast to his own experience. The four sections taken together suggest that Verdicchio is writing a long prose poem which unites into one coherent whole the vast, varied experiences (fatherhood, the son, Italy, and life and death in Canada). "Father" is one large travel trunk (Italians call it *baule),* packed with a wide assortment of images and experiences, past and present.

The first section begins with the poet returning back to Italy thirty-three years after his father emigrated to Canada. The poet is slightly older than his father ("three years older than you were then") and tries to reclaim his Italian citizenship that somehow was lost: therefore "a foreigner in the land I was born." The loss of Italian citizenship contributes to the poet's identity puzzle and to the over-all feeling of loss and disconnect "First Death" tries to address.

My mind is always not here. My body feels alone. My emotions without a place to root, have settled on the surface of my skin.

Living and working in the city of San Diego at the university is no comfort nor is its temperate climate and endless sunny days a cure for alienation. When the poet's father suddenly requires a medical operation, he is called back to Vancouver, his original city (a personal Eden), where the skies are a perennial grey for weeks (sometimes months) and "the landscape is lush and seductive." The return plunges the poet (and us) back into the past when he worked as fire-fighter and how his father faithfully drove him to work every day. Here is memory: "a sudden surge of huge clouds", "we were soon engulfed in mist and rain and thunder." Memory appears and centres the poet, taming his unnamed longing and evoking his former work place as a psychic harbor.

The father's operation is successful — the removal of cancerous tissue — but it is here we arrive at one of the central concerns of this section of the poem. Inheritance is not simply a matter of citizenship; it also includes the question of "unwanted inheritance": "What do we do with [cancer] now that is has been handed down to us?" Verdicchio observes that "cancer is the ultimate virgin birth, a clone of one's genetics, a cesspool of humanity."

During a visit at the hospital, he realizes upon looking at his father asleep in the recovery room that his body resembles his father's. The corrupted body is where the immigrant past continues to live in the present. The past represented in the living flesh of the present. The poet's skin: "The pattern of moles around his neck, shoulders, and arms are the ones I recognized in myself when I entered my forties . . . My whole life I have been told I resemble my mother." The past asserts a physical presence in the present: "something there that calls out to me now."

The body's physical past as a kind of document of the immigrant experience continues in "Final Death", the second part of "Father". Here, the poet studies his father's watch now on his arm: "When I look at the watch, I see your arm, not mine . . . The watch is forever inscribed with the image of your arm and body."

Verdicchio gathers evidence of the physical past mediated by and through his father's present body. As he begins to photograph his dying father, he writes about his thoughts and details what he is doing. He becomes a witness to his father's life and death, but also to himself as son and photographer/poet. The photographs document Verdicchio's interior journey as much as they are an archival record of his father's looming death: "Each photo is an attempt at finding myself in which I see brothers, cousins, grandparents, even my own children but not myself."

Verdicchio's journey is a reckoning about the relationship between father and son, about his own relationship to his own children, and about how the past and present are psychologically fluid: "Father, Papa, Babbo, Baba, I wonder where we are. These names draw us close to and through each other. What I call you, my children now call me: Babbo."

From the photos Verdicchio takes and the text he writes, it clearly emerges that he is searching for a revelation, a meaning, something to which he can attach sense and significance. This section closes with potent questions: "Does the image of a person change after emigration? What do the eyes tell? Is there a difference in a body in time? . . . How does one change when migrated away from one's self?"

The final note in this section describes Verdicchio's father in military uniform, in 1947, walking down a street in Naples: a handsome figure captured by a photograph. Also present is a street vendor and a poster of a Hollywood movie on a wall. All the elements combine in the photograph and emit "the Future". But the future takes time to answer the present; the future is the present waiting to happen.

"Dreams After Death", the third sequence of "Father", as the title points out, is a series of dreams, one different from the other, events and images merging into each other. This poem opens with the narrator/poet carrying two bottles of wine the way his father did, "the neck of one bottle between the index and middle fingers and the butt of the other resting on the ring and little fingers . . ." His father waits for him at an underpass: a waiter in a Neapolitan restaurant. Then the setting changes. We are in a garden and this scene, in turn, changes again, and we find the poet safe, pressed against his father's body: "dream traces the geography of his being." The whole dream sequence is a series of transformations, one scene moving into another until it becomes apparent dreams are memories and memories are dreams, the distinction blurred. "I can't quite tell if there is a boat out there. If there is, it is a memory of it."

Notions of time, setting, travel, people walking in and out of the frame of a dream, behave in ways we expect in dreams. What is noteworthy is all the dreams evoke images of family, the need to connect to family, a train going South, and of course all are set in Italy.

"Father" concludes with "Postscript". The old family neighbourhood in Naples has been transformed by gentrification. The poet carries the commemorative cards of his father's death and, as he walks through the familiar streets, he cannot help but notice they have changed. He wishes to hand out — a gesture of love — some cards on the street, but in the end he concedes that the transformation is such that he concludes: "I found myself holding your photograph, glad to be carrying you with me."

The present is an imperfect container. It cannot receive or hold what the poet remembers. Better to hold onto the memory of what was of his father than deal with the past transformed.

With "Father" Verdicchio examines how memory, photographs, and dreams interact in the ever-shifting ground of identity, expressed and preserved (captured) by the pale, crystal amber juice of words.

The three poems discussed here demonstrate Pasquale Verdicchio's concern in the body, place, and memory, and in how each interact to create imagery. Poems provide a fresh understanding of the immigrant experience and the poet's experience of dislocation.

Work Quoted

This Nothing's Place: Selected Poems. Toronto: Guernica, 2007.

LEONARDO BUONOMO

THE POETRY OF PASQUALE VERDICCHIO

1

In the Name of the Farther

IN CRITICISM ON North American authors of Italian background one often observes a regrettable tendency to think of the writers' identity as an arena, or a battleground, in which opposite forces vie for supremacy.[1] The Italian side, it is almost invariably assumed, is the weaker of the two, doomed to be ultimately defeated and conquered. Since the confrontation is staged on American soil, time is believed to be the American side's most powerful ally. Year after year, generation after generation, the Italianness of the Italian North American author is destined to lose strength, to become more and more diluted, until it is hardly recognizable. What remains of it will occasionally reemerge here and there, peeping out, as it were, in the form of place names or references to food, amid a sea of Americanness.

The scene of Italian North American writing, however, is far more complex and varied than this. It extends from the early travelers, adventurers, and missionaries of the seventeenth, eighteenth, and nineteenth centuries, to the immigrants of the 1880-1920 period and those who followed in later years, and includes the current expatriates: students, academics, artists, who live and write in North America. Pasquale Verdicchio embodies this complex, multi-faceted character. His identity and his poetry defy simple, clear-cut categorizations.

Born in Naples in 1954, he moved to Canada in the late sixties and since 1980 has been living in Southern California, where he teaches Italian literature and writing at the University of California, San Diego. He is the author of several collections of poetry, numerous essays (some of which have been collected in the volume *Devils in Paradise*), and has published translations of the works of, among others, Antonio Porta, Pier Paolo Pasolini, Giorgio Caproni, and Alda Merini. Reading his books of poems in succession, from *Moving Landscape* (1985) to *Approaches to Absence* (1994), one cannot but notice how the foreign, Italian, Neapolitan element in his verse, far from receding, has progressively gained prominence, affecting not so much his subject matter, as the verbal and syntactic texture of his writing. The longer he lives in North America, it would seem, the more hybrid he becomes. Although Verdicchio's poetic trajectory is sometimes hard to map (which is fitting for one who identifies with the figure of the nomad, as he does), there is no doubt that he has been moving away from Standard English usage and forms. His desire to "contaminate"

English with other languages, as he put it in a recent essay (*Devils* 38), is much more visible in his recent poems than in his early ones. Indeed, in his first book *Moving Landscape* he seems intent, for the most part, on getting the most out of the aural resources of English alone, on releasing the "magic of the pure sound of words" (to use Jakobson's and Waugh's expression, 247). One recognizes this in his pronounced taste for alliteration, and his propensity for the rounded phoneme "w", which gives a lovely aerial quality to "Red-Winged Blackbird" (the poem that opens *Moving Landscape*). As they form the words "wind" and "wing", the lips open outwards, as if the words themselves were on the point of taking flight:

> Wind. Wind
> and wings of birds.
> A red-winged blackbird
> sparks against the sky
> and green shrubs;
> comes to rest in the safety
> of calls that break
> against our words,
> clear and intelligible words,
> and light the evening
> with the fire of meaning (11).

The poet's passionate commitment to language is given form and substance in the text by the physical, tactile presence of "words". Words are "clean and intelligible", like a crystal or, given their inflammable nature, like a fragment of flint. In this and other poems of *Moving Landscape* the stuff words are made of suggests a hard, inorganic material, that needs to be scraped or shattered to produce meaning. In the poem "Letter", for example, we read of "another place name fallen/to the page, its letters broken/to mean a thousand words" (12). Besides the concreteness, the tangibility of words, the image suggests a dissemination of signs, to be gathered and reassembled to form new words, as one would do with the pieces of a puzzle or a mosaic. We can also be reminded of a kaleidoscope, in which no pattern remains the same for long, for words are very much a part of the shifting scene, the moving landscape of the title.

At times the impression is that the landscape (and everything in it) is conceived of as an immense manuscript that needs to be deciphered. Everything is "text": the fish in the sea, the human body, the fossils of extinct animals, the remains of ancient civilizations. In such an environment it is small wonder that the poet's senses need to be constantly on the alert. For even a hyperactive gaze such as his could not do justice alone to a scene where sound can take on the properties of light and light those of sound, as in "Between the Desert":

The sea. Not the sea.
Music reaches out from towers:
notes reflected in the eyes of women.
Desires, already memories,

encrusted with onyx and agate.
A traveler arrives, misunderstands
the redundance that fills his eyes:
always leaving, always returning,
he finds himself between the desert (19).

Sound is also, constantly, the protagonist of Verdicchio's poetry at the textual level, as in that teasing opening line, with what might be a faint echo of Hamlet's famous question, or in the poem "Ritual", where sibilants hiss like the wind: "The curtain on his door whispers / its movement in the wind. His / hands reach high into branches, / spill silent into the air: / a conversation . . ." (28).

In an interview given a year after the publication of *Moving Landscape*, Verdicchio describes one of his central themes: the idea of the writer as traveler. "To write is to migrate, to be in constant movement" (*Devils* 135), says Verdicchio, and this assertion is convincingly supported by his evocation of the figure of Ulysses in the poem "Artaud and Nobody":

During his great voyage
he changed his name to reflect
the seas he had traveled,
names of his experience.
To everyone he came to be
known as what the one-eyed visionary
had called him: Nobody.
Nobody returned home
to find he had never been there
and his name, usurped by words,

found its way across centuries
becoming over and over the traveler:
man searching and finding himself
tied against songs of mermaids
and temptation . . . (34).

No less relevant are Verdicchio's references, in this and other poems, to Dante, a poet-voyager himself and one of the supreme creators of the myth of Odysseus.

Verdicchio's 1990 book *Nomadic Trajectory* could be seen as a poetic rendering of those theories of rootlessness and distance that, according to Arjun Appadurai, are needed to deal with "the world we live in now" (122). Literally placed at a distance from his first two worlds, Italy and Canada, the California-resident Verdicchio has felt an affinity for the rootlessness of the nomad and the idea of movement between places, rather than from or to places, associated with that figure. Living and working in a sort of neutral ground, Verdicchio himself embodies a condition of in-betweenness, of transition between languages and cultures that finds expression in his poetry and translations.

Comparing *Nomadic Trajectory* with *Nomadic Landscape*, one observes in the former a considerable increase in Latinate words and unorthodox syntactic forms, and an extremely frugal use of punctuation. The latter feature is especially worth noticing in that, in a way, it gives the act of reading itself a "nomadic quality". We proceed unfettered from line to line, with that peculiar sense of freedom we experience in the absence of a pre-established direction or destination. As Rosi Braidotti has pointed out, "the nomadic traveler is uniquely bent upon the act of going, the passing through", and is a figure that is well attuned to the "transitional movement that marks our historical situation" (12). To adopt the "nomadic garb" allows Verdicchio, and us as readers, to resist "assimilation or homologation into dominant ways of representing the self" (Braidotti 12). The attractiveness of an unpredictable, nomadic trajectory becomes all the more apparent if we consider under what pressure so-called ethnic writers are to limit themselves to a pre-established set of themes and images in exchange for recognition from the dominant culture.

Disappointing those critics who expect the "hyphenated writer" (Italo-American, Chinese-American, etc.) to strew his or her text with "ethnic crumbs" (so that *they* can find the way), Verdicchio alludes to his origins and his "expatriate" status with admirable discretion and indirectness. As Emily Dickinson would have put it, when Verdicchio tells his story, he tells it slant. Thus in "Branta Candensis" the change of scene, the passage from one land to another, from one language to another, is almost entirely devoid of realistic details.

A mouth full of names before the leaving
people at the open border:
nothing and nothing to fear.

Come expecting never again the transparence
the sweetness of discourse;
not what it started out to be,
understand opposition:
Cut from past experience of
secrets revealed to hands and eyes
kept from fleeing with the view
the horizontal window of music
When the geese flew overhead
I could not help but think
of what lay north (10).

In "Parthenope" a montage of voices, languages and different stylistic registers suggestively mimics the multi-layered historical texture of Naples, and gives an unconventional, unsentimental character to this revisitation of the poet's native city.

Gulf sweeping arm to comprehend
from Capo Miseno to the tip of
Punta Campanella, protected by the heights
rising with the unmistakable outline of Vesuvius
citizen recounting the stories of others
A grid of dissimulation the city impervious
the shell of fiction: transferring metonymical placement
an identity claimed by so many places
one city yet all possible cities
in fragments . . . (12).

A few poems in *Nomadic Trajectory* are divided into numbered sections one may think of as successive "removes" in the nomad/poet's travel narrative. The journey motif is further emphasized by the titles of four poems – "Between the Desert", "Encampment", "Oasis", and "Within Landmarks" – which form a sequence bearing the same name as the entire collection. In these compositions one detects, in addition to the aforesaid division in chapters, a "laceration" in the middle of the page, a blank space separating two uneven, jagged columns of text (which can even be read "vertically", as lists of words). This unusual structure induces the reader to pause, to look first at one "pile" of words, than at the other, before choosing his or her course. We thus become one with Verdicchio's poetic persona and his concern that:

> . . . the ignorance of points leads astray;
> we choose
> the paths assessing significance
> Movement takes place   and always always
> between before and after
> Exile constant
> for the nomad
> who has every
> and no place

> ("Between the Desert" 33).

The poet's interest in the "question of language", an expression that may refer both to the history of Italian culture and to the current situation of post-emigrant writers such as himself, creates a link between *Nomadic Trajectory* and Verdicchio's 1993 book *The Posthumous*

Poet: A Suite for Pier Paolo Pasolini. The Figure of Dante, evoked in the long, composite poem "The Arsonists" (which closes *Nomadic Trajectory*), is followed in the later collection by those of Pasolini and Gramsci, whom Verdicchio has repeatedly acknowledged as major influences on his work. Like Dante, both Pasolini and Gramsci reflected on the linguistic heterogeneity of their country, a problem that has followed Italian immigrants to North America and other parts of the world and that continues to be relevant in today's Italy. The question of the interaction or superimposition of languages and cultures becomes visible on the pages of *The Posthumous Poet* in the form of translated titles of Pasolini's works and quotes from Gramsci. So does Verdicchio's strategy to infiltrate, in his words, the structure and "ideology of the [English] language" with Italian elements (*Devils* 145). At the aural level these presences may be said to produce a ventriloquial effect: the sound of voices coming from elsewhere and joining that of the poet.

Heretical Empiricism. Where the poet stands. As a result of his body it extends well beyond. Language of the spectrum of non-dominant forces. Dried blood of miracles liquefies yearly. Inhabit the curvature of the Earth. At a point of preliminary observation. Are they not narrative structures homologous to capitalism? The geography of ideology well defined; the role of the intellectual. Free indirect discourse.

Overcome obstacles by force
of love, do not knock them down, but loosen them
like the action of water on soil.

*

Every hegemonic relation is necessarily pedagogic (49).

The Posthumous Poet begins in a prayer-like tone ("In the language of the mother/in the language of the son/offer us a simple past/in place of an uncertain present" 11) and ends with a section (entitled "The Crucifying Code") that suggests a dirge or a requiem. It is only here that the violent death of Pasolini is explicitly mentioned ("the body of the poet battered by murderers" 61), but the whole composition – which I think is meant to be read in one sitting – may be said to lead up to that line. Not only is the idea of death introduced since the very title, but scattered among the lines are terms like "assassins," "wounds", "lacerated", "murderous", "torture", and "executioner", that flash images of suffering and the brutal suppression of life.

But posthumous, by definition, is what remains after death, what, in a way, preserves a dead person's voice. The posthumous poet is then the poet who has survived his own physical decease, whose body is now the text of his works, which we may continue to study and interpret.

[93]

Verdicchio's poetry is at its most abstract and cerebral in *Approaches to Absence,* published in 1994. As in *Moving Landscape* and *Nomadic Trajectory,* Verdicchio is still very much concerned with place and movement, but these categories have been stripped of almost all familiar connotations. Indeed, everything is so removed from common experience that one can get heady from the rarefied air emanating from Verdicchio's lines. Interestingly enough, the book includes a revised version of a sequence of poems titled "A Critical Geography" that was originally published as a chapbook in 1990. What clearly emerges from a comparative analysis of the two versions is that Verdicchio's guiding principle in the revision has been one of subtraction. A considerable number of words, and sometimes whole lines, have simply disappeared in the later edition. One notices that it is mostly objects belonging to the sphere of quotidian experience that have vanished from the scene. "Tile roof", "bicycles", "casements", "letters", "shoes", and "canvas" are only some of the casualties of Verdicchio's ruthless editing. It may very well be that this "distillation" of reality is one of the "approaches to absence" to which the book refers.

In another section called "Translatio" the space where one would expect to find words is occasionally occupied by straight lines, arrows, dots, and signs that look like vertical dashes. Here reading poetry is as much a visual as an auditory experience. In addition, one can think of these signs as yet another language (after English, Italian, and Latin) being added to the poet's rich repertoire. "Translatio" indicates the transfer of something (words, for example) or someone from one place to another, from one context to another. And what is most valuable to Verdicchio, once again, is the transition itself, rather than the points of departure and arrival. The process of translation is particularly liberating for expatriates, Verdicchio suggests, in that it empowers them to explore their duality or multiplicity, without having to identify entirely with a single culture.

> The condition of expatriates who must write mutely
> out of step constant readjustment intrinsic
> and extrinsic to the act of writing
> to fall in step out of step
> tangential provocation of linguistic expression
> an eye off to the side
> keeping acculturation under watch
> translation is not becoming
> but (di)versifying (57).

"My house of language," Verdicchio acknowledges later in the same poem, has "no walls" (60). It is perhaps a mobile home that is always on the move and which has cruised through all the developments and experimentation of his craft. Sometimes his readers may find it difficult to keep up with its speed and its sudden, daring turns, but if they manage to hang on to it they may be carried along in a fascinating journey.

2

Home Is Where the Word Is

Reading Pasquale Verdicchio's recent poems, collected in *This Nothing's Place* (2008), one finds confirmation of what was suggested by the last two sections of his 2000 book *The House Is Past*, namely that this self-styled "nomad" author has finally found a home, at least on the printed page. (The first six sections are a reprint of poems published between 1985 and 1994). After years of moving steadily and boldly towards various forms of experimentation with language (or rather, *languages*, given his enrichment of English with Italian words and syntax) as well as with sound and typography, Verdicchio seems to have arrived at a place where he can work simply, blending together everything he has learned.

In his 1994 book *Approaches to Absence*, Verdicchio's writing kept the promise of the title with elliptical, abstract lines in which the sound, and the placing of words on the page, appeared to take precedence over meaning. Movement had been the leitmotif of his poetry from the very beginning, but in his continuing exploration of the resources of language, Verdicchio seemed to have wandered off into an uncharted territory where both he and the reader came very close to losing their bearings.

By contrast, in many of the poems included in *The House Is Past* and *This Nothing's Place*, Verdicchio appears to make of his art the key for entering (or re-entering) — and taking possession of — sites both geographical and metaphorical: the cities of his childhood, youth and maturity, as well as the scenes arising from his memories and cultural heritage. Paradoxically, even when the emphasis is on loss (both cultural and personal), what emerges most distinctly is a sense of belonging, of rooted-ness, that finds expression in the sheer abundance of words variously related to reassuringly enclosed spaces such as "room", "residence", "house", and "home." Such is the case, for example, with the poem that opens the penultimate section of *The House Is Past*, the poignantly titled "Casualties of Memory":

> Given a map of relative strangers
> somewhere a face opens the world.
> It is called home,
> from a distance.
> I said somewhere.
> I mean here (136).

The pleasure the poet takes in the familiar is so palpable it belies the funereal imagery of the first part of the piece, with its references to casualties "wrapped in soiled kerchiefs . . . [burning] without scent" and a site that "repeats the chant of mourning" (136). Memory is also invoked in the next poem, "Abitino", whose very title conjures up images of childhood and parenthood. With its incantatory, nursery-rhyme-like cadences the poem suggests a cross between a child's cooking recipe and a magic spell, which intends to congeal time, to preserve it from spoiling:

> a pinch of ash, a pinch of salt,
> a pinch of cornmeal,
> three grains of salt,
> three of pepper, the hair
> of a black dog, the figure
> of a saint;
> A strip of paper with a word
> or two to hold in memory.
>
> (*House* 137)

The universal child evoked by these words becomes a particular child in "Mara Moving through the House", dedicated to, and named after, the poet's real-life daughter. Here the speaker acknowledges, and takes comfort in, the intimate connection between the familiar domestic setting and the human figure who passes from room to room transforming the space around her, colouring it with her presence:

> A small area of flight
> delineated by a smile;
> empty rooms fill behind you.
>
> (*House* 138)

In "The Corner of My Eye" the poet returns home, literally, by revisiting Naples, the city of his birth. The poem is divided into two stanzas, each opening with the image of a hand in motion, beckoning, as it were, the speaker to the realm of his memories. In the first stanza it is apparently the hand of a stranger that invites him (and us) into the sensorially charged interior of a room in the Old Spanish Quarter, the densely populated maze of streets and alleys at the heart of the city:

> A hand from a window …
> pulls into a room
> walled by the scent of
> freshly brewed coffee accompanied
> by the clink of glasses
> in which the dark liquid smokes.
>
> (*House* 140)

A metaphor for the city, where its preparation and consumption is a ritual, coffee here affects all five senses with its colour, heat, taste, scent, and the sound of glasses. So the first stanza continues:

> Hands reach out to the smoke
> and lift the glasses to the lips
> that will later speak
> of its flavour and kiss
> the living atmosphere
> of the brimming city.
>
> (*House* 140)

Madeleine-like, the flavour of coffee ushers us into the memory of family ties and gestures in the second stanza, in which the perception of the "hand" is now a moment of recognition:

> your hand.
> The hand of a sister,
> cousin, a relative hand
> that cannot be halted.

(*House* 140)

Its touch can revive moments and experiences that seemed lost forever. It is a haven for what is worth preserving of one's experience and the receptacle of "all thoughts and dreams" (*House* 140). To get in touch with the past can also be a way to distance oneself from a disheartening present, as suggests in "The Swimmer". Contrary to our expectations, that process is envisaged not as a movement backwards, but forwards, while the present stands for the danger lying in "what has been left behind" (*House* 147).

Verdicchio's collection *This Nothing's Place* owes its intriguing title to a passage in Canadian writer and painter Emily Carr's book *Klee Wick* (1941). Recalling a walk she took on Vancouver Island's west coast, Carr tells how, while treading "a strip of land that belonged to nothing . . . neither to sea nor to land," she found her way blocked by a "fallen tree [that] lay crosswise in this 'nothing's place'" (27). Given Verdicchio's multicultural identity and experience (Neapolitan/Italian/Canadian/Californian), his "place" may be equally elusive and hard to identify, and yet what his new poems convey, more so than the ones which preceded them, is Verdicchio's need to connect with a "strip of land" of his own, made up of his heritage, memories, and art.

In the opening poem "M" (the initial of Mara, and the month of May mentioned in the first line), the poet observes his daughter observing, and taking in, the world. It is through this shared visual act, a form of communication in which light and colour take the place of words, that the bond between them is first suggested. Seeing is soon accompanied by gesturing and hearing in the interplay between father and daughter:

> a coloured headband
> and a smile half-hidden
> behind a self-conscious hand.
> The silence of your body.

(This 9)

But it is the language of the body that finally emerges as the most profound, and eloquent, means of expression through which the poet conveys his feelings:

> then you ask
> about the space

that has opened in me
and I can only answer
with a gesture that means you.

(This 9)

Family ties, roots, the matter of perception, and the need to come to terms with one's place in the world recur as some of Verdicchio's primary concerns in the poems "Sight" and "I Am a Fixture". Even though, as a poet and critic, he has always been acutely aware of the various cultural components that make up his "entwined background", to borrow an expression Helen Barolini has used for Jewish American writer Letty Cottin Pogrebin, and that find expression in his use of language, Verdicchio is never facile in his treatment of his hyphenated identity (106). Thus, for example, in "Sight" he can perceive the smothering quality of Italian family relationships and, at the same time, the keep-your-distance quality of their non-Italian counterparts:

Unlike us, they see the value of strings
that can be tethered
to hold one distant.
We use those ties
to reel each other in,
to bind us too close for sight.

(This 16)

In "I Am a Fixture" the world of Italian American director Martin Scorsese, evoked through his name and citations from his films *Taxi Driver* and *Goodfellas*, is stripped of any nostalgic quality and used as a misleadingly familiar setting for an enigmatic reflection on the acts of creating and writing. Startlingly, the process by which a blank sheet of paper is filled out with words is associated with images of violence and bloodshed. If not mightier than the sword, the pen in this poem is just as deadly:

> but you take the pen
> and stab the guy over and over
> and I cringe at the thought
> of being written on
> with a pen stained in blood
> dipped into the body of a man
> and then dragged over my surface.

(*This* 34)

Even though Verdicchio's recent poems still display, to some extent, his penchant for hermetic pronouncements and the delight he takes in the sheer pleasure of sound, one notices a new confessional quality about his writing, a new selfless urgency to leap into observation and simple emotion. Nowhere is this more evident than in the long closing section entitled "Father", a poignant prose elegy in which the poet renders into words his experience of, and response to, his father's illness and demise. Divided into three parts ("First Death", "Final Death", and "Dreams After Death"), and followed by a postscript, this section opens with the poet transatlantic back in Naples, where he and his father were born. It is now thirty-three years after the latter's "crossing" and the poet is "three years older than [his father was] then" (*This* 65). What Verdicchio recreates here is indeed a journey back in space and time and one that requires him, as it were, not simply to revisit his father's life and examine his own deepest feelings for him, but to *become* his father. Verdicchio recalls how in the course of his visit he discovered, much to his surprise and dismay, that he had lost his Italian citizenship and, like all non-European foreigners wishing to live and work, even temporarily, in Italy, he had to apply for a visa and a permit of stay, a predicament, one suspects, not too dissimilar from the one his father must have found himself in upon arriving in Canada. But the twist, in Verdicchio's case, was that he had returned "home" only to become, to all effects and purposes, "a foreigner in the land where [he] was born" (*This* 65). What is more, his quintessentially Italian name puzzled those who examined his situation, in that it did not fit with his alien status. As William Boelhower put it, "[i]mplicit in one's family name is a story of origins, a particular system of relations" (81). In Verdicchio's case, however, it was as if that implied content had been erased.

Fittingly, this almost surreal experience introduces us into what is, essentially, an exploration of identity. A flash-forward brings us to San Diego, California, the poet's place of residence and work for many years now but never, really, his home, "a city that remains foreign and unsettling" (*This* 66). It is there that the news of his father's life-threatening disease reaches him. To complete the list of places that, in different ways and measures, can claim to have made Verdicchio what he is today, we then move to Canada, the country of his adolescence and young adulthood, as well as of his citizenship.

The place that houses this other part of Verdicchio's life is Vancouver which, in stark contrast to the emotional remoteness of sunny, dry San Diego, is "a city that seeps into your body like the humidity of its long rains" (*This* 67). Vancouver stirs memories of familiar haunts and, most tellingly, glorious outdoor work with its accompanying sensation of the pure pleasure of being alive, just when the reason for the poet's visit is the delicate operation his father has to undergo in a local hospital, "a visit different from any other, a visit that required an accounting of all our lives" (*This* 68).

For all the relief he feels following the successful surgical removal of a malignant tumour from his father's colon, the poet cannot help thinking of this phase as a merely temporary respite and pondering on both the symbolical connotation of cancer, "the ultimate virgin birth, a clone of one's genetics . . . It emerges out of us and engulfs us, smothering us in our own cellular matter" and his own mortality (*This* 70).

Looking at his father in his hospital bed, Verdicchio tries to make out the contours and lines of the strong man that the shrunken, frail, vulnerable body meeting his gaze once was. It is, in a sense, a form of reading, an interpretation, which is why, perhaps, Verdicchio accompanies it with a playful echo of T. S. Eliot's "The Love Song of J. Alfred Prufrock": "In the room the nurses come and go, talking of Mario, a patient etherized by life upon the table" (*This* 71).

The sound of the common Italian name Mario, so incongruous a replacement for the illustrious Michelangelo of the original, anticipates a moment in which Verdicchio is forced to consider another aspect of his father's legacy: leaving the country of one's birth and creating a new life where one's native language is experienced as extraneous, as a mark of difference. A doctor making his rounds feels the need, upon entering Verdicchio's father's room, to adjust his register, to simplify it, as if he were walking into a miniature version of Vancouver's Italian neighbourhood:

> He was outside talking to the nurse and when he walked in to talk to us there was a perceptible drop in his diction . . . His assumption must have been that an accent means a lack of sophistication about certain things, and definitely a lack of linguistic sophistication and expressive potential. Odd how at the end it's like at the beginning, how the sum of our long residence in this country is still drawn to signify foreignness (*This* 75).

Returning to his reading of his father's face and body, Verdicchio tells how he gradually discovered, as he grew older, how much he resembled his father. Having been told all his life that, as regards physical appearance, he took after his mother, it was only when he reached his forties that he began to recognize his father in himself, not his facial features but rather his frame and posture: "There is something there that calls out to me now. I resemble you, Babbo, in perhaps more subtle ways. I resemble you in the shape a body takes with age" (*This* 77).

It comes as no surprise, then, that when at a later stage in this section Verdicchio puts on his father's gold-colored watch, the arm he sees in front of his eyes is his father's, not his. The obtrusive ticking of the old-fashioned watch introduces the account of Verdicchio's father's last hours and the poet's need to recapitulate the dying man's life by describing photos of him taken throughout the years. As he puts it, each "photo is an attempt at finding [himself]" (*This* 83). And indeed, when Verdicchio muses on whether the images taken after his father moved to Canada reflected his new status or some undefined quality that signalled a new phase in his life, he is also trying to gain deeper insight into his own identity: "Is one's bodily difference a result of age or distance from one's former self, one's other self, a self more recognizable and familiar. How does one change when migrated away from one's self?"

(*This* 84). The mirror-like quality of the relationship between Verdicchio and his father does not end with the latter's death. It comes back to haunt the poet in his dreams where it is further emphasized by the concurrent presence of Verdicchio's son Giuliano. Thus, in a richly evocative dream sequence Verdicchio sees himself walking with his son in Italy, but the people who greet them take them to be his father and himself. So does, movingly — and startlingly at the same time — Verdicchio's own mother, imagined as she was at eighteen: "The dream ends with a feeling of lightness and perplexity, the fresh and clean smell of her dress, the brightness of the sun and her smile" (*This* 89).

In the postscript that closes the "Father" section, and the book, Verdicchio is once again back in Naples, literally retracing his father's steps. After playing with the idea of leaving one or two commemorative cards with his father's photo in places his father might have liked, or in the familiar streets of his neighbourhood, the poet cannot bring himself to do so because the places have changed.

The last possibility of leaving the cards anywhere is the central station where he is to catch his train. However, "as the train pulled out of the Napoli Centrale, I found myself holding your photograph, glad to be carrying you off with me" (*This* 94).

That powerful parting image, one feels, is a fitting metaphor for Verdicchio's homage to his father's memory, for the way in which, as *This Nothing's Place* eloquently demonstrates, it found its warmest and safest home in the poet's writing.

Note

1. I chose the last line of Verdicchio's "Fact/Confession" (*Approaches* 17) for the title of this essay because it admirably sums up his poetics, his endless fascination with movement, his eagerness to explore new forms and styles.

Works Cited

Barolini, Helen. *Chiaroscuro: Essays of Identity*. Madison: The University of Wisconsin Press, 1999.

Boelhower, William. *Through a Glass Darkly: Ethnic Semiosis in American Literature*. New York: Oxford University Press, 1987.

Carr, Emily. *Klee Wyck: The Emily Carr Omnibus*. Vancouver: Douglas & MacIntyre, 1993. 15-86.

Eliot. T. S. "The Love Song of J. Alfred Prufrock." *The Waste Land and Other Poems*. London: Faber & Faber, 1981. 9-14.

Verdicchio, Pasquale. *Approaches to Absence*. Toronto: Guernica, 1994.

———. *The House Is Past; Poems 1978-1998*. Toronto: Guernica, 2000.

———. *This Nothing's Place*. Toronto: Guernica, 2008.

KENNETH SCAMBRAY

ON THE POETRY AND ESSAYS OF PASQUALE VERDICCHIO

1

The Outsider As Devil

WHAT WE SOMETIMES forget in the era of the printed word is that poetry is also aural: it must be heard to be fully appreciated. At first glance, Pasquale Verdicchio's poetry on the page appears more a puzzle for the eye than sounds for the ear. But something happens to his linguistic montages when read aloud. Some years ago, at a reading at my university for my Italian American literature class, my students responded with an intuitive awareness of what his poems meant. More important, they also grasped immediately that the poems should be allowed to speak to each listener or reader individually. They did not strain for a single reading of each poem. They were open to the possibility of legitimate, alternative interpretations. They allowed that Verdicchio's poems opened a discourse rather than begged for a specific meaning. The interpretations of his poems inhabited the space someplace in between each listener. Even with its sometimes puzzling, unconventional syntactical usage, Verdicchio's poetry still strikes the listener viscerally, where we expect all poetry to affect us.

But the visceral response for the listener is only just the beginning of sorting out what Verdicchio's poems can mean to the listener and reader. In fact, that visceral response is where the trouble begins, as it is intended, in his poetry. Troubling is a good word to describe his poems' devilish linguistic form. Like my students' responses, ultimately, it is in between the heart and the mind where the important battle rages. His poems locate the reader in a landscape that remains forever combative, ever changing, and unsettled. Verdicchio believes that the personal war, the conflict over identity, as well as the cultural war, history and politics, should be perennially fought out, but never settled. He says in his interview with Antonio D'Alfonso, in *Duologue:* "The immigrant is the outsider as devil, disturbing the waters of paradise" (92).

According to Verdicchio, the ethnic writer should never seek official sanctification. In his judgment it is the mainstream that we must fear, the seduction of ethnic writers from margins into an assimilated conventional identity that erases their history and individuality. Verdicchio does not so much fear a society that veers either left or right. To him it makes no real difference. His concern is that all societies ultimately aim to create an all-consuming and repressive cultural center.

This is what distinguishes Verdicchio's poetry from the history of twentieth century poetry in English and much of North American Italian post-immigrant poetry. In their poetry, the influential modernists, such as T. S. Eliot, Ezra Pound, and William Carlos Williams, however different their intentions were, intended to establish in their poetry and theory a definitive space, politically, culturally, and linguistically. Verdicchio's poetry is intended to roil the cultural and personal waters, to defy any hardening of both personal identity and the cultural center of North American society. To him, standard syntax is another form of tyranny. Standard English could not serve his end. As he explains in *Duologue*: "My activity, therefore, is aimed both at English and at standardized Italian. I am trying to find, not that I want to write in dialect, but I need to find a language in which I am able to express my condition" (32).

Though he is fluent in Italian, his immigrant and migrant condition happens mostly in English. Therefore English became his language of choice. But Italian is still at the core of his identity. The major influence on his poetry is the Italian poet Andrea Zanzotto, whom Verdicchio has translated. Zanzotto spent a lifetime experimenting with poetic form and dialect. At the same time, he had a profound interest in history, as Verdicchio does. In Zanzotto's enigmatic verse, Verdicchio sees an assault on the conformity that twentieth-century Italian culture intended to impose on the individual, politically and linguistically.

A major part of the history that informs Verdicchio's poetry is a reflection on his immigrant past and his childhood in Naples, as well as how that past continues to inform his present life in North America, from Vancouver to San Diego. But when readers, especially North American Italian readers, read his unconventional poetry, his chiseled, multifaceted lines do not contain those stereotypical ethnic signs. They are bereft of the usual nostalgia for that boyhood past in what should otherwise be an idealized Neapolitan landscape. Missing also are those iconic images of a sentimentalized immigrant family life. Those signs of the immigrant's struggle in the face of a repressive Anglophone culture are also absent in his poems. Verdicchio does admit that nostalgia, the emotional return and attempted reckoning with the past, can be a legitimate starting point for the ethnic writer. He says in *Duologue*: "Ethnic writers have certain themes and subjects to talk about, mostly nostalgic ones. That stage must be recognized and addressed. Unfortunately . . . the nostalgic mode tends to take over both the writers and the critics. That is what institutionalized multiculturalism requires of the so-called ethnic or minority groups" (81).

Even multiculturalism, which in its inception was supposed to liberate the ethnic writer from the oppressive mainstream culture, suddenly creates its boundaries and its own center, demanding that all ethnic writers abandon the margins and speak in a unitary cultural voice.

Instead, what Verdicchio advocates and has in fact done is to use nostalgia as a way into his poetry, but not as the all-consuming focus, emotional and intellectual, of his poems. Otherwise, Verdicchio says it will "bog you down in the past" (*Duologue* 82). Nostalgia is just a first step. He argues in *Duologue* that it must become "a way to . . . politicize your contemporary existence" (82). The past, including his personal past, is certainly in his poems. History and his personal past become even more pronounced in his last book of poems, *This Nothing's Place*. Nostalgia should just be the beginning of a writer's reflection on personal history. Verdicchio argues that if it is allowed to become the sole aim of the writer, it erases important aspects of the personal and ultimately the more important political struggle of North American Italian writers that should be represented in their work.

In his nomadic odyssey from Italy to Canada and finally to the U.S.A., as he explains to Antonio D'Alfonso in his interview, Verdicchio asked himself, who am I: Italian, Canadian, or American? As he explains to D'Alfonso, everything that he did in North America had to be filtered through language, first through the Neapolitan dialect of his youth, then standard Italian, and finally English. He had to wrestle constantly with how he was going to maintain his dialect, the rootstock of his cultural and linguistic heritage, while on his odyssey through both standard Italian and English. He resisted the social process that attempted to push his Southern Italian identity toward that Anglophone and WASP cultural center in both Canada and America. But as he explains in *Duologue*, this process "is the illusion that you can just shed who you are, take the clothes of culture off and walk naked into acceptance and assimilation. As if somebody is going to hand you a different set of clothes, clothes that are going to represent a different version of history and of who you are. You end up wearing what others want you to wear, without even getting to accessorize on our own. That is the problem" (57).

As both a dialect-speaking Southern Italian and immigrant in North America, Verdicchio is uniquely positioned to understand how all ethnics are stereotyped in society and ultimately intimidated into adopting a linguistic and social conformity. As an Italian citizen, Verdicchio understands how social conformity is not only a violation of personal rights of the individual, but also a grave political threat to North American society, in fact to any society anywhere in the world. Rather than discovering in his poetry and scholarship nostalgia for his boyhood past, what we find instead is a problematic representation of history. In his quest over the last forty years to define his identity in North American society, he also discovered the historical and political reasons behind his immigrant odyssey to North America. He came to understand why his family immigrated to Canada in the first place in the 1960s. Though he remains "bound" to his Italian origins, he is aware of modern Italy's many political and cultural problems. The post-war period before the 1970s in Italy is an era that has been vaingloriously labeled Italy's great "economic miracle". But the economic growth in the post-war era that created Italy's now well-established middle class did not extend into the beleaguered, impoverished South, including Naples. In *Duologue*, he asks, "[w]hat did the economic boom do for so many southerners?" (83). In his introduction to Antonio Gramsci's *Southern Question* and in *Bound by Distance*, he discusses the North's exploitive economic and cultural policies toward the South in the decades after unification. He discovered that like millions of other southern Italian immigrants, his family was forced to emigrate or be mired forever in the South's stagnant economic pool, not to mention the criminality that today grips Naples. The South's economic and culturally inferior position was not an accident. Rather, it was the result of the North's well-defined economic policy that prohibited the industrialization of the South and reduced the South to little more than a labor pool for northern industrial development.

As he explains in *Bound by Distance*, Verdicchio's in-between cultural position that he inhabits as an ethnic in North America is rooted in the fascism and racism that characterized Mussolini's reign. In fact, he explains that the racism against Southern Italians has a long history in unified Italy and predates even Mussolini's reign. As he says in *Duologue*, suddenly he realized that "My dialogue was not only against Canadian nationalism, but also against Italian nationalism. That is why I cannot accept all the claims rising from *Italianità*. Not only did I feel deracinated in Canada, but I felt that the reasons for my lack of roots were a result of the Italian sociocultural reality. It wasn't only Canada imposing its culture, but I felt I had been exposed to that imposition as a result of Italy having imposed its own terms on me as a child. If we agree that history has not ended, that we are a result of and live in history, how can anyone then deny their background?" (99). He goes on to say that "[e]ven though Italian culture in the post-war period is mostly left leaning or influenced, the institutions of fascism are still very much present. Pasolini talked about them, and his talking about these issues led to his assassination . . . We have Italian parties in Italy that are examples of fascism. Fascism is not over" (59).

Left or right, the cultural center remains a constant threat to the individual's identity. Verdicchio's poetry, in its content, language, and form, is a resistance to a "fascist" mentality, that centripetal social force that draws everything and everyone in society toward the center. As Verdicchio wrote in *Bound by Distance*, in the context of cultural studies, "The terms 'American' and 'European' refer to standardized cultures that are in fact rather narrow in scope. Similarly, the use of 'Anglo' . . . functions as a cultural negation when used to describe invisible minorities within its purview" (137-38). In the face of this constant cultural challenge, Verdicchio's poetry exerts a centrifugal cultural force that is "catastrophic". It destabilizes and threatens the stability and dominance of the cultural center.

Nevertheless, in his poetry, Verdicchio is on a quest for a home, but not the conventional home reflected in the nostalgia of most ethnic poetry. Inescapably, he feels that he is "bound by distance" to his past. But that Italian past is problematic, one that has, for better or worse, shaped his identity. His home, whether in Italy or North America, cannot be the traditional home of settlement. If the "house is past", that place where his identity is rooted, it is a personal and cultural space that remains forever conflicted. His family's emigration was necessitated by northern Italy's unjust social policies that relegated the South to a cultural and economic backwater. The only armchair in that home is one that inhabits a conflicted space, characterized by social injustice and racism. At the same time, while his identity is rooted in that past, it is "absent" in his North American wanderings. His current condition becomes for him a "nothing's place" that offers no clear resolution to the conflicting cultural trajectory of his nomadic intellectual and emotional wandering as immigrant and migrant. But in his poetry and other work, Verdicchio's problematic cultural position is not intended to be a negative commentary on his resettlement in North America. Rather, the titles to his poetry books, his non-standard English grammar and the unconventional form of his poems are a call to resist that inevitable centripetal drift of all societies, from Canada and the U.S.A. and to Italy, with Mussolini's continued influence on contemporary Italian politics. Left or right leaning, the centripetal cultural force of democratic societies will always be a threat. His unconventional syntax and poetic form are a sign of what he feels must be his obligatory position on the margins of North American culture. In defense of his cultural position, in "Communication Called Passage," he writes, "A language of purity / is the sign of a dirty conscience" (*The House Is Past* 123).

2

Culture, Identity, and Language

The House Is Past: Poems 1978-1998 is a selection of Pasquale Verdicchio's poems published over the last twenty years from six of his previously published works. Most critics have always had difficulty locating Verdicchio's poetry in the tradition of North American Italian poetry. Verdicchio's poetry captures the itinerate physical and emotional life of a poet who has lived in between cultures and national identities since his departure from Naples, Italy, as a boy.

Immigration and migration, settlement, and resettlement recur as themes throughout the poems in the volume. History and remembrance are as well subtexts in his poems, but not in the conventional way we expect to find these themes in North American ethnic poetry. In both its form and content, at first glance it does not appear to conform to the textbook definition of ethnic Italian American poetry. His poems lack those stereotypical images of family, neighborhood, relatives, food, and other iconic signs that have become nearly *de rigueur* in ethnic poetry. Nevertheless, Verdicchio's poetry qualifies as among the most probing and insightful statements on the bicultural experience in North America.

Verdicchio's poetry captures the essence of the bicultural experience in both the style and content of his poetry. With Italian writer Antonio Porta among his chief influences, Verdicchio challenges conventional notions of language, identity, and culture. He breaks down traditional syntax. Many of his poems cannot be read in a linear manner from left to right.

Whole poems, such as "Within Landmarks", are composed of fragments or phrases: "Waterless soil visit/ image of the desert/at random in rocks/remember landmarks/female figures." On the page, these images are juxtaposed with one another. How should they be read: up or down, left to right, or right to left? There is no correct way to read the poem. However, his unconventional syntax and images add up to a certain impression in the reader's or listener's mind. But the impression cannot be and is not intended to be necessarily the same for everyone.

The form that his poetry takes is consistent with the concepts his poetry expresses about history, culture, and personal identity. The titles of his previous books, from which these poems are selected, reveal the themes that are at the center of the bicultural, North American Italian experience: *Moving Landscape*, *Nomadic Trajectory*, and *Approaches to Absence*.

Verdicchio attacks all centrifugal, unitary notions of culture and identity. For him, as an Italian, a southern Italian, Italian Canadian, and Italian American, he has been on the "move" intellectually and physically. He has been on a "nomadic" quest to fill with meaning the "absence" of his past and heritage in the "trajectory" of his evolving and ever-changing life in North America. His poems exemplify that universal ethnic condition of being forced to live in between.

As a Canadian and American Italian, he has lived on the margins of the culture wars between the Quebecois and English in Canada and in between the constructed notions of "white" and "black" culture in American society. Complicating the cultural conflict, the voice in his poems is caught in between the past and present: the North American present and the Italian past. The past remains a constant presence in his poetry: the house is past. Home in his poetry is present and past. Yet for the Italian ethnic voice in his poems, settlement will always remain problematic.

Coincidently, Verdicchio reveals in his most recent collection, *This Nothing's Place*, that he inexplicably lost a few years ago his Italian citizenship. His confusing and bizarre quest to reclaim his Italian citizenship through the Italian bureaucracy is an appropriate metaphor for the uncertainty and instability that defines the modern immigrant experience. Further adding to his woes, at the same time, while living in Southern California, questions arose about his Canadian citizenship and passport. Suddenly, his connection to his birthplace and his land of resettlement was in question. He found himself nearly bereft of any national moorings, in Italy, Canada, or America. It is just this condition of absence and nomadism that his early poetry captures both in the general immigrant experience over the last one hundred and fifty years and prophetically in his unstable personal and cultural condition. As he says in "This House, That House," "Not enough to leave quiet home life behind,/still one has to ask: / Where has everyone been diverted to?" The problem of immigration and its aftermath, for both immigrants and their offspring, is that of where and how to find a comfortable cultural space to call home.

But Verdicchio does not seek for that place of comfort, that place of cultural and personal stasis. That he says is only a fiction. Rather, as his poetry implies, any constructed, unitary notion of identity or culture is dangerous, for both the individual and the state. Cultures and societies around the world are in constant flux. In "Moving Landscape," he writes, "I am the only man missing/from the landscape/of ready-made history." That is not the plaintive cry of a victimized voice, but rather the antithetical position in which the ethnic consciousness prefers to reside in society. In fact, Verdicchio prefers his position on the margins, a place where he can successfully resist any form of imposed identity. "Ready-made" history is that repressive unitary notion of culture that all societies attempt to create and that is designed to identify the "other": all those marginalized in society by fictitious theories of race, gender, and culture.

In Verdicchio's poetry, the cultural reality is that, as he writes in "The Cutting Edge", "[t]he landscape is moving." In "Branta Canadensis" the migrating Canadian geese are compared to "A mouth full of names before leaving/people at the open border." The voice in the poem concludes, "When the geese flew overhead/I could not help but think/of what lay north." The indefiniteness of the cultural experience lies in what Verdicchio calls "discourse" in the poem. Conflict is the reality of all cultural identities, not their constructed unitary notions of cultural identity. In "Oasis," images of "encampment" always give way to "marshes", "known landmarks" to the "wandering village", the "wayfarer's knowledge" to "perilous rovers in the field", "in a new land" to "foreign voices", and "impatient thirst" to "rainwater". In "Fragmenta" Verdicchio writes that the idea of a "simple past" is juxtaposed with an "uncertain present" and "moved totalities". Settlement always leads to resettlement in a continuum of problematic personal and cultural changes.

There is never a sense of resolution in Verdicchio's poetry. There is no sentimentality in his poems, no resolution of the bicultural conflict between the present and past. Even the past is subject to revision. As Marino Tuzi has written, nostalgia for the past is a masking of the emerging and often conflicted ethnic self. Creating a discourse is at the basis of everything that Verdicchio writes. There can be no center. Conventional syntax is tyrannical: it forces all speakers and readers to see and hear in the same manner. Conflict emerges through the tension that his unconventional syntax causes in the reader's mind. To unify cultural values and irreconcilably fix them from a specific historical perspective is, likewise, tyranny. This is what happened in Italy under Mussolini. This same impulse in American culture to define one religious and ethnic tradition – WASP — as the origin of American cultural identity has marginalized the ethic voice among us for generations.

As Verdicchio's poetry dramatizes, the only place for the ethnic voice is that antithetical position between cultural places: neither one nor the other. In both the content and the syntax of his poetry, tension and conflict are never resolved. As a result, tyranny remains at bay in its influence on both personal and national cultural identities. As Antonio D'Alfonso argues in *In Italics*, discourse creates an obligatory cultural instability. There is always space for a new voice and a new perspective. A chair must always remain empty at the cultural round table. We never know what nomadic soul may come through the open door. As Verdicchio says at the end of *The House Is Past*, "The search for water is the divination of language. Begin digging where the story bends."

3

The Dissonant Subject

Devils in Paradise: Writings on Post-Emigrant Cultures includes fourteen essays and three interviews with Pasquale Verdicchio conducted by Canadian Italian writers, Dino Minni, Sergio De Santis, and Rodrigo Toscano. Verdicchio's disparate essays and interviews are unified by his successful effort to draw new boundaries for North American culture and to redefine the individual writer's relationship to a new reterritorialized and decolonized cultural landscape. The "devils" in our North American "paradise" are what Deleuze and Guattari in *Kafka: Toward a Minor Literature*, call minor writers. Minor writers' works are marginal in any cultural hierarchy in both form and content. Out of necessity, they even remain on the margins of our now institutionalized multicultural society in North America.

In Verdicchio's view, the role of the minor writer is to attempt to weaken the cultural center — whether it be French, Anglo-Saxon, or multicultural — and to open society up to discourse and greater freedom for the individual, politically and culturally. In his view, multiculturalism has recreated a new center, a new hierarchy of race or ethnicity. Central to everything that Verdicchio discusses is the cultural identity of the minor writer who consciously works to avoid serving any "master" in society.

In "Subalterns Abroad: Italian Canadian Writing Between Nations and Cultures", Verdicchio argues that the emergence of Italian Canadian writing is a reterritorialization of Canadian culture and a disruption of the politically expedient and artificial binary culture war between the French and English.

The basic problem in Canada is linguistic. Alienated from language and culture, the so-called minority writer in Canada creates a space between the Anglophile and Francophile factions in Canada. In occupying this space between these two factions, Canadian culture is forever changed. Whatever that minor writer produces, it is not within the conventional context of either the Anglophile or Francophile social environment, of class, culture, and language. The writer's production remains radically political and de-centers Canadian cultural discourse.

No longer can the French of Quebec and the English simply focus their cultural discourse exclusively on the presence of each other in their binary cultural war. French separatism is no longer separatism from just the English. Rather in their quest to re-center Quebec linguistically, socially, and culturally, they must now realize that even if they succeed, they must deal with the minor writer within their separatist boundaries. Excluding just the English does not solve their culture war in the face of the panoply of languages now spoken in Canadian society.

Verdicchio argues that when Italians, or any of the other immigrant or post-immigrant cultures in Canada, use either French or English, depending on their geographical location, they are not necessarily re-locating themselves culturally in either faction. They are merely practicing what Verdicchio calls "post colonial adaptation", what is now an important aspect of our post-colonial and post-immigrant world. He cites, for example, that French and English are the national languages of many African nations, while these countries remain singularly dedicated to creating unified and viable cultures based on African and not necessarily French or English models. As Verdicchio points out, Nigeria's Chinua Achebe, Somalia's Nuruddin Farah, and Shiva Naipaul have all adopted their former colonialists' languages in their writing without compromising their national identities or the ability to articulate accurately the post-colonial problems that their cultures face.

Similarly, though they may use English or French, Verdicchio argues, Italian Canadian writers must break from the linguistic and cultural forms of the dominant Canadian (bi)culture. Italian Canadian writing must seek its own voice and place in Canadian culture and break both the creative and cultural silence that has for over three generations surrounded Italian Canadian writing. He argues in "Subalterns Abroad" that Italian Canadians must "re-instate" themselves into not only contemporary Canadian society, but into North American and European history as well. They must take stock of what forces drove them from Italy in the first place and what forces in Canadian society continue to marginalize them and deny them a voice in Canadian society.

In "The Borders of Writing" Verdicchio is careful to point out that the intention is not to redefine North American Italian culture for the purpose of creating a new center. Institutionalized multiculturalism is as bad if not worse for minor cultural awakening than the hegemony a centrist culture exercises over history and discourse. Similarly, in "A Non Canon" he argues that the Italian canon in North America should work from "an ambiguous situation of resistance" to centrist culture. The efforts of North American Italian writing should "be not [a] movement towards equivalency" (107). In Deleuze and Guattari's words, minor writers should actually cultivate their marginalization status because it affords them the "possibility to express another possible community and to forge the means for another consciousness and another sensibility" (17).

Vying for the center in competition with other ethnic writers is nothing more than a variation on the established "rule of state" that already exists in U.S.A. and in Canada, including what the *Québécois* would like to achieve with their separatist, nationalistic ideology. Verdicchio would agree that it is the role of such writing to address the center in an effort to keep it from solidifying national identity under one banner, whether it is Anglo-Saxon, Puritan, French, or otherwise. In other words, writing from the margins and maintaining a revolutionary, destabilizing relationship to the cultural center does not isolate or make the minor writer irrelevant in the cultural process.

However, Verdicchio points to one group, Italian intellectuals and poets who immigrated to America in the "post-1968" period, who are content to remain on the margins with their poetry and prose, which does not challenge the hegemony of either America's "white" Anglo-Protestant heritage or the equally imaginary new multicultural center. In their comfortable academic positions in Italian departments throughout the country, these post-war Italian immigrants, in Verdicchio's view, are equivalent to the

French separatists of Canada. By writing exclusively in Italian for their Italian audience, mainly in Italy, their writing does not tilt or challenge centrist notions about American cultural or personal identity.

In their academic positions, they continue to maintain a separatist position, refusing to identify with Italian Americans. They insist on writing in Italian, thus separating themselves from both the Italian American community and American society at large. Yet many have lived in America for decades and some are even ignored in Italy. They hold themselves aloof and have, as a result, defined for themselves a separate class and cultural category from earlier Italian immigrants to North America and their post-immigrant offspring. Though they write voluminously, they are content to remain on the silent margins, not the revolutionary margins that contribute to, in Deleuze and Guattari's words, the "break-down" of centrist hegemonic culture.

Verdicchio's answer to the complex questions he raises is to create a heterogenous view of experience in his poetry. Taking, for example, Andrea Zanzotto as a model, he creates in his poetry a form that challenges the conventional syntax, iconography, and usage of conventional writing in both English and Italian. Thus, he carves out for himself that minor place in his cultural production that remains in-between, but not passively so. His poetry is a political statement in what its form and content enunciate about history, culture, and identity.

His unconventional tropes and syntax undermine the conventional ways that "major literature" has historically represented culture and identity. Unlike other professors of Italian in North American universities, Verdicchio's decision to write in English is also a political and cultural statement. His poetry is a radical commentary on the hegemonic center of culture, whether in Canada, U.S.A., or Italy. With Zanzotto as his major influence, his Italian birth, and Italian as his first language, it could be argued that Verdicchio's poetry is also Italian. Should language be the only criterion used to assign cultural and national identity? Verdicchio says that his writing "is a stageless formation of dissimilar poetics offering a multipolar critique of our Canadian and Italian realities" (38). While his poetry is certainly personal and historical (a point that is too often denied by his critics), it does not repeat or, in his terms, regurgitate conventional images and nostalgic landmarks of village and *paese* that have become obligatory in ethnic poetry over the last century.

Verdicchio explains in "A Poet in A Moving Landscape", one of the three interviews in *Devils*, that "My identity crisis, my search for roots takes place in language. I don't write to find out if I am really Italian or Canadian, or to express my anguish at having to leave my native land. I write to question" (135). He tells us that "I do not want to be told that my reality is an 'immigrant experience'" (136). His poetry will not be circumscribed by the colonialist linguistic structure (even if he does use English) nor by conventional, nostalgic ethnic writing. In "The Borders of Writing", he comments on the reception of his poetry:

> the silence regarding my writing on the part of the Italian Canadian writing/critical community is directly related to institutionalized 'multiculturalism' and its influence on the prescription of ethnic identity. It designates value according to predefined themes. To act upon language in such a manner, while not denying the historical basis of English or Italian, alters the languages so as to emphasize the presence of external or dissonant subject. The alteration of English syntactical sequences, the insertion of Latinate terms, verses or words in Italian, Neapolitan, Latin, are all meant to instigate a cultural temblor (38).

In William Boelhower's terms in *Through a Glass Darkly*, his poetry "explodes" all stereotypes and conventional approaches to identity. His writing is a radical commentary on centrist assumptions about culture, identity, and language. Even more important, because of his poetry's "syntactical sequences," it cannot be drawn comfortably into the center. It is poetry that serves no master.

In Verdicchio's view the categorization of people in institutional multiculturalism only increases social problems and tensions between ethnic and so-called racial groups. It is just another form of what he calls "historical erasure." In America the simple binary Canadian culture war between the Anglophile and Francophile factions is reproduced in the equally simplistic and self-serving "white" vs "people of color" description of American society. The American sign "white" also finds its equivalent in the new term "Euro-Americans." While this tidy, unhistorical binary division of American culture into only two factions may empower "people of color", it disenfranchises all other minority cultures, just as it does in Canada. Colonized for centuries and denied a voice in the modern Italian state, southern Italians emigrated, and now they and their descendants are denied both their history and voice in contemporary American culture.

In "Tracing the Ground of Identity: Ethnicity and Race in Women's Narratives," he finds fertile ground in the works of Mary Bucci Bush, Dodici Azpadu, and Mary Melfi on which to reconstruct avenues of communication and similarity between Italians and other groups. Implicit in these works is an attack upon centrist culture and even the new "institutionalized multiculturalism," which only serves to divide ethnic groups against each other.

In Bush's work set in Mississippi, Italian immigrants and African Americans work on a plantation together and share the hardships of their subaltern lives. In Azpadu's "Desert Ruins" she explores the extermination of the native *Siculi* in Sicily. In Mary Melfi's work the "'black' immigrant" stands in contrast to the white, assimilated middle-class woman. Both Madonna — *nata* Ciccone — in her videos and Camille Paglia in her essays on culture and gender challenge comfortable assumptions associated with upper-middle-class feminism. Paglia argues that Ciccone's dark brooding sensuality is not only derived from her Italian roots but even finds its parallel in the sexuality typically associated with African American culture.

More could be said here, as well, about the vital role that first and second generation Italian American youth played in the 1950s and 60s in the development of that subversive popular form, Rock and Roll, with its roots in Rhythm and Blues. Verdicchio further cites Rose Romano's struggle to assert her Sicilian heritage within her lesbian community, where Jewish and Italian are summarily categorized as "white." But Verdicchio argues that in these women's narratives we can see that easy ethnic categorization is not possible. In the trajectory of their work connections can be made to other groups and together they can stand in opposition to centrist culture and institutional multi-culturalism that threatens to erase the history of Italians to simplify centrist cultural definition.

In "Fante's Inferno" Verdicchio finds in John Fante's enigmatic fiction a struggle for identity in the face of the pressures to assimilate. In his Los Angeles novels, Fante's main characters struggle to be accepted into mainstream society. But Verdicchio argues that, though Bandini never directly addresses his Italian American identity in his struggles, he is a profoundly polarized writer. He lives in between his identity as an Italian American and his dream to assimilate and become a famous American writer. Verdicchio sees this self-loathing acted out in his conflict with and abuse of his Mexican girlfriend.

This abuse, Verdicchio argues, is a form of self hatred because of his "non-identity as a 'real American'," which he shares with his ethnic girlfriend. At the basis of his Los Angeles novels is a main character, who has, in his far western setting, attempted to erase his history. Nowhere in any of the novels does he mention the Italian communities that surround his hotel on Bunker Hill. He is the colonized ethnic in crisis. He struggles within himself to find his identity, and when he sees it before him in his Mexican girlfriend, he is filled with a sense of attraction and self-loathing.

Verdicchio traces this Italian immigrant self-hatred to its roots in Italy in the racist works of "Cesare Oombroso, Afredo Niceforo, Giuseppe Sergi, and other positivist 'scientists' of the turn of the century, who defined southern Italians as inferior beings along with Jews and Africans . . ." (57). Though Verdicchio does not mention them, these Italian "scientists" found their American counterparts in the influential works of eugenicists and nativists, such as Madison Grant (Yale, Columbia), *The Passing of the Great Race* (1916), Theodore Lothrop Stoddard, (Ph.D, Harvard) *The*

Rising Tide of Color Against White World Supremacy (1920), William McDougall (Ph.D, Cambridge), *Is America Safe for Democracy?* (1921), Ole Hanson, *Americanism Versus Bolshevism* (1920), and Charles W. Gould, *America: A Family Matter* (1922).

In their books they argued for the limitation or the exclusion from the U.S.A. of the inferior Asian "races" and Southern European "races". The range of opinions in the works extended from Hanson's argument that immigrants could import seditious ideas that threaten to undermine democracy to eugenicists' argument that unsavory Asian and Southern European races would vulgarize America's Aryan stock.

Lest we think from our twenty-first century point of view that these writers were extremists speaking to an equally fringe group of Americans, it is worth noting that William McDougall was an English immigrant and a noted psychologist who held the William James Chair in Psychology at Harvard. Two had Ph.D.s while Grant earned a B.A. from Yale and a law degree from Columbia. Hanson, the son of Norwegian immigrants, was the mayor of Seattle and the founder of San Clemente, Calif. Furthermore, four of the books were published by Charles Scribner's while Hanson's book was published by Doubleday. These publishers published some of America's most important novelists of the period.

These writers, especially Grant, were the engine behind The Johnson-Reed Immigration Act of 1924, which successfully established exclusion categories and quotas for what the United States government considered undesirable aliens. The basic premise of the act was to exclude those "races" that the government felt would compromise the American racial stock or would undermine American cultural values: family, democratic, political, moral, religious, and educational. The act specifically targeted Asians, Eastern Europeans, and, above all, Southern Europeans, especially Italians.

Over eighty-five percent of the Italians entering the U.S.A. were from the South. Being the largest immigrant group to enter America at the time, at an average of more than 200,000 immigrants per year from 1900 to 1921 (excluding the war years), Italians were specifically targeted. Unknown to most cultural historians, to stop the alarming rising tide of "colored" southern Italians, the U.S. Congress hastily passed an Italian restriction law in 1921, limiting Italians to 46,000 immigrants, a reduction of approximately 77% of the total. The 1924 act finished what Congress had done in the 1921 law by further limiting the Italian immigrant quota to little over 3,800, from the original 200,000, a reduction of 98%.

In "There Dago!" and "If I was six feet tall, I would have been Italian" Verdicchio discusses the denigrating images of Italians on television sit-coms and in Spike Lee's urban films. He finds in Lee's films more than Lee himself intended to portray. Verdicchio points out that Lee unconsciously portrays that Italian

Americans and African Americans share similar backgrounds. Both southern Italians and African Americans historically have suffered from the stigma of "racial" inferiority. Eradication of their respective and collective histories has led to their sometimes-open warfare in urban America.

The real problem according to Verdicchio that the Sicilian boys have is not, as Lee would have us believe, their racism born of their assimilation into "white" society. Rather, what Lee seems to have missed is that they inhabit the same subaltern class in urban America that their parents and grandparents inhabited as *contadini* in Sicily. Their real problem is that their "blackness" has also been repressed by the impoverished circumstances in which they find themselves in an oppressive and exploitative twentieth-century capitalistic urban environment with African Americans (80).

Rather than understanding their historical connection to their African neighbors, the American class system denies their heritage to them and requires that they become the enemy of anyone who inhabits their subaltern class in American society. Their anger and frustration is focused on the wrong segment of American society. In Lee's caricature of Italians, they become invisible and their real history obscured, something that African Americans can understand. The southern Italian boys' conflict with African Americans in Lee's films finds its parallel in a similar but bloodier conflict in Los Angeles over the last thirty years between African American and immigrant and post-immigrant Hispanic gangs.

In other short essays Verdicchio calls for North American Italian critics to write their own criticism. In "The Failure of Memory in Language" he addresses on the same theme of the need to know history. He writes that Italian Canadian writers must begin the process of "historicizing dialects in the context of emigration and Italian national culture" to better understand the past. Even so he argues in "Non Canon" that a common language of North American Italians must be English. However, Verdicchio cautions writers that the placement of Italian words in texts creates only the illusion of belonging to a community. Yet he explains in "Crossing Place", the final interview in *Devils*, that as a bilingual writer he attempts in his poetry to "infiltrate English with Italian". The appearance of both Italian and other languages in his poetry serves as signs not of nostalgic memory fragments of his immigrant experience but of his efforts to create a hybridization of cultures, which all cultures are in reality. This is yet another way of de-centering culture, weakening it and thus making it open to discourse and ultimately change.

Verdicchio proposes a radical redefinition of culture. He fears, and rightfully so, that in institutionalizing multiculturalism contemporary North American society has created a new center and news margins. Multiculturalism has created a new "racial" hierarchy, relegating North American Italians' identity to the non-descript "Other" on racial profiling census and polling forms. However, the complexity of Verdicchio's view requires that North American Italian writers should not clamor for a place in the multicultural center, but should remain on the margins.

The North American Italian writer's role is to be the dissonant subject, to create a discourse and fashion a social order that will always remain open to new voices. Whether in a French, Anglo-Saxon, or multicultural society, North American Italian writers must become aware that their history and identity face historical erasure.

As he says about the relationship between his own poetry and his reader, the North American Italian writer must work to create a space for voices and relationships other than those officially prescribed by institutionalized social and cultural definitions. Ultimately, the minor writer must do the "devil's" work in exploding stereotypes, breaking down centrist cultural icons, and obscuring rigid cultural definitions that delimit both the identity and freedom of the individual.

4

The Decontextualized Subaltern

Bound by Distance: Rethinking Nationalism in the Italian Diaspora is a comprehensive work on the dialogue that Pasquale Verdicchio believes is necessary between Italy and North American Italians. It is Verdicchio's contention that both Italy and North America have not done enough to facilitate a discourse over the influence and meaning of Italian immigration. Furthermore, Verdicchio contends that such a discourse will not only aid in our understanding of immigration, but it will also aid in Italy's understanding of its long-debated "Southern Question".

For North American Italians, revisiting their Italian past will bring them a better understanding of the complex cultural position that they occupy between Italy and North America, as well as their location in the current discourse over race in America. To borrow Verdicchio's title from his collected poems, the "house" that North American Italians currently inhabit must be reconciled with its conflicted Italian "past".

For many decades Italy did not acknowledge the existence of the hundreds of its immigrant Italian colonies around the world. The reason for this, Verdicchio argues, is that Italy has never confronted the internal social and cultural problems that caused that massive immigration of southern Italians to North America and other parts of the globe. It is widely understood even in Italy that the mass immigration that occurred from the South was the manifestation of serious economic problems in the South.

By 1945, more than twenty-six million Italians emigrated to various parts of the globe. By 1924, the

U.S.A. had admitted 4.5 million Italians, 85% of which were from the impoverished South. But even more important to Verdicchio, and less widely understood, even by Italian Americans, is that the mass immigration that occurred was also the result of equally serious cultural problems in Italy.

It is a telling historical fact that within a generation of the unification of Italy in 1870 and the overthrow of centuries long foreign domination, millions of southern Italians left their homeland. Why wasn't this a time for rejoicing and hope for the southern Italian peasantry?

As Verdicchio points out in his opening chapter, "The South as Dissonant National Subject", southern Italians were not necessarily supportive of unification. After years of subjugation by foreign governments, the French and Spanish Bourbons chief among them, southern peasants were not easily swayed by what they perceived as yet another hegemonic force from the North.

As Verdicchio writes in the subsection of his chapter entitled, "The Risorgimento and The Exclusive Nation: Unification as Colonial Subjugation," the southern peasantry had every reason to be suspicious of any northern invading army, even if it began in Sicily under the leadership of a liberator with the name Giuseppe Garibaldi. Verdicchio reminds us of the well-known racially inspired saying still relevant today in Italy, "Italy ends at Rome. Naples, Calabria, Sicily, and all the rest are part of Africa." Or there is also the widely circulated racist remark: "Upon unification of the North with the South, Africa lost half its population."

In the remainder of the section, Verdicchio delves into great detail on the failed economic reforms and other political shortcomings of the unification government that never delivered on its promises to the southern peasantry. He also explains that, in its quest for a unified state and culture, the North has overlooked the southern peasantry's reasons for resisting the unification of Italy. The notion of a unified, monocultural Italy, Verdicchio argues, is a myth that hides not only Italy's true cultural diversity, but also cloaks the cultural divisiveness and fundamental inequality that continues to exist even today between the North and the impoverished South.

In a recent publication, Verdicchio's thesis is supported by Pino Aprile's *Terroni: Tutto quello che è stato fatto perchè gli italiani del sud diventassero "meriodionali"* (Milano: Piemme, 2010). Aprile argues that upon the unification of Italy, Piedmontese troops did not liberate the South from Bourbon colonization. Rather, the North invaded and subjugated the South to yet another foreign power. In his chapter entitled *"La Strage"*, Piedmontese troops raped and killed southerners, crimes which have never been officially acknowledged by Rome. As unwilling subjects of the North's efforts to unify the South, southern peasants also suffered extensive damage to their property, for which villages have officially demanded reparations, which have never been paid by Rome. Worse, he argues that in the wake of unification, the South became an economic and labor resource for the North, excessively taxing the South's economy and forcing the South's young people to migrate north solely for the enhancement of northern industrial development.

It is worth pointing out that *Bound by Distance* precedes and anticipates several other recent studies on the subject of Italian identity: *White Upon Arrival: Italians, Race, Color, and Power in Chicago, 1890–1945* (2003) by Thomas A. Guglielmo; *Are Italians White? How Race is Made in America* (2003) ed. by Jennifer Guglielmo and Salvatore Salerno; the less nuanced, *Working toward Whiteness: How America's Immigrants became White: The Strange Journey from Ellis Island to the Suburbs* (2005) by David Roediger; and an excellent study of the Piedmontese in California, *Terra Soffice Uva Nera: Vitivinicoltori piemontesi in California prima e dopo il Proibizionismo* (2008) by Simone Cinotto. All of these works take up the subject matter that Verdicchio addresses in his work, especially the complex subject of race.

At the basis of the southern Italian identity problem, as Verdicchio explains in another subsection of the same chapter entitled "The Question of Race", the North held well-defined racist views against all southern Italians. Verdicchio writes that "[f]ar more influential than post-Unification southern resistance to annexation in the contemporary North/South debate have been the works of positivist anthropologists" who argued that Southern Italians were racially inferior to Northern Italians. At the end of the nineteenth century and the beginning of the twentieth, several "scientists" constructed racial categories based on their false reading of Darwinian evolutionary theory in which southern inferiority became an unquestioned "scientific fact."

One of the most often quoted books was Giuseppe Sergi's *Ari ed italici* (*Aryans and Italics* 1898). Sergi argued that southerners are descendents of Africans and posits the theory that the two distinct Italic "races", northerners and southerners, are so different that unification of the Italian population would be impossible. He went on to argue that northerners had a greater affinity for culture and civilized behavior than southerners. Sergi and his other supporters would find their ideas complemented in the United States by, among others, Madison Grant's *The Passing of the Great Race; or, The Racial Basis of European History* (1916), and Theodore Lothrop Stoddards's *The Rising Tide of Color Against White World Supremacy (*1920). These works were highly influential in the passage of the 1924 exclusion law, designed to stop the flow of eastern and southern European and Asian immigrants into the United States. These same pseudo-scientific racial theories would also appear later in both Hitler's and Mussolini's racial laws.

Though Verdicchio hastens to point out that some Italian intellectuals did come to the defense of southerners at the time and have continued to do so over the decades since the war, as Aprile's *Terroni* also points out, their arguments have never been enough to eradicate from Italian culture this racist division between the North and the South. Northerners' prejudice against southerners remains even today the only truly indigenous form of racism that exists in Italy. Racism remains alive and well in the politics of Umberto Bossi and The Northern League which seeks to divide Italy in half. The only possible difference is that Bossi wants Rome to be a part of the South.

In Chapter two, "The Subaltern Written/The Subaltern Writing: Standing Figuration of Southern Cultural Expression", Verdicchio deals with the location of the southerner in Italian culture. He discusses the manifestations of racial stereotypes, especially Neapolitan, that persist in Italian culture today. He treats the question of how the subaltern peasant can find a way of speaking and becoming a contributor to "official" culture. As Verdicchio points out, Pier Paolo Pasolini, in his poetry, prose, and films, is one of the most important commentators on the exploitation of the subaltern subject in Italian culture. Pasolini made a connection between the subaltern subject both within and outside Italian society, between the cultural position of the southern Italian and the colonized in places such as Africa. Pasolini's *The Savage Father* (Guernica 1999), translated by Verdicchio, is an interrogation into the psychological and social effects of British colonization in Africa. Pasolini saw a connection between both internal and external forms of colonization.

In Chapter 3, "Bound By Distance: The Italian Immigrant as Decontexualized Subaltern", Verdicchio gets closer to home and to the application of the commonality shared by all Italians, those who remain in Italy and those who, even generations removed, share a cultural connection to Italy in the Diaspora. Verdicchio writes, "[t]he impact of the massive movements of Italian emigration has yet to be fully recognized or assessed" by both the Italian government and scholars in Italy and abroad. By implication, immigrant and post-immigrant North American Italians have yet to assess the continuing influence of those racial laws that marginalized them and their ancestors in southern Italy. What influence does the cultural position — both economic and racial — that drove so many southerners to abandon their homes still have on their cultural and economic position today in North America? How has gaining acceptance into middle-class life reshaped their view of themselves, African Americans, and other more recent immigrants?

Verdicchio sees a common cultural bond that continues to exist between Italy, Italian immigrants, and their second and third generation descendants, everywhere in the world. In spite of the great success of Italian immigrants abroad, Italians still maintain that common prejudice against immigrant Italians and their descendants. It is not hard to understand why. More than 85% of Italian immigrants were southerners. Verdicchio points out "that certain dismissive attitudes are still very much at work in how emigrants are regarded" in the study of emigrant literature in Italy. Verdicchio argues that Italians, including Italian Americans, must acknowledge this fundamental problem in their marginalization in the historical process in both Italy and North America.

According to Verdicchio the cultural bridge between Italy and its "colonies", as well as between the North and the South in Italy, is in the writings of Antonio Gramsci. Born in the impoverished region of Sardinia, Gramsci was among the first Italian writers to understand that fundamental cultural rift that divided the North from the South. He articulated the inherent racism that formed the northerner's view of the southerner. Verdicchio argues that not only does Gramsci help us to understand the "Southern Question" internally in Italy, he helps us to understand the cultural position of the North American Italian immigrant as a "decontexualized subaltern" abroad.

As subaltern subjects, Italians as ethnics in both Canada and America share a similar role in the national cultures as the southerner does today in Italy.

Verdicchio would even argue that they share this position even in their more advanced stages of cultural and economic assimilation. This is manifest in Verdicchio's view by not only North American Italians' lack of understanding of their subaltern, Italian heritage in Italian culture, but also their problematic identification with official culture. As Verdicchio points out, wherever they may live, in Italy or North America, "Southern Italians have always straddled the categories of white and nonwhite, a situation that served the racist purposes of the nationalist movements in Italy as well as those of the ethnic purists in the U.S.A. and Canada."

As Gramsci points out, the South as a colonized region never developed an indigenous intellectual class that could articulate its position historically in Italian culture. The North's economic exploitation of the South and the mass migration of its young people drained both the South's coffers and its intellectual reserves as well. Similarly, it has taken North American Italians more than three generations to create that intellectual class needed to reposition them in both Canadian and American cultures. While negative stereotypes of Italians abound, for too long North American Italians have watched in both frustration and silence, not really knowing how to respond.

Verdicchio goes on to give examples of the untenable position of North American Italians, from their absence in the bipolar British/French conflict in

Canada, to their categorization as "white" in the Black/White racial polarity in America exemplified in the films of Spike Lee. However, Verdicchio rightly believes that such a simplistic bipolar definition of culture and race is masking of the true complexity and diversity of North American Italian subjectivity. For example, in Spike Lee's *Jungle Fever*, regardless of what might have been Lee's intention in the film, Verdicchio believes that there are "various crossover relationships within the film" that challenge the simplistic, stereotypical black/white dichotomy on the surface of the film. As the cultural and historical products of their subaltern peasant heritage, Italian American men share a greater affinity with their supposed black antagonists in the film. Verdicchio argues that this is a cultural position that Lee refuses to grant, at least consciously, to his Italian American subjects in the film. By implication, of course, Verdicchio is arguing that Italian Americans, confused over their own "racial" history in both Italy and North America, readily accept Lee's obliteration of their historical position as the subaltern subjects of both racial and cultural inferiority.

In the final chapter, "A New Way of Being Gramscian", Verdicchio analyzes how Gramsci's theories can help in deconstructing the totalizing cultural façades that both racism and consumerism have created in modern society, in both Italy and North America. Referring again to both Gramsci and

Pasolini, Verdicchio argues that folklore, for example, is not an inferior cultural product, but the legitimate cultural expression of subaltern people. Since historically they have been denied the creation of an intellectual class, their voice must be understood in its various manifestations and injected into the national discourse over culture.

Verdicchio analyzes recent manifestations of popular, folk culture in the international hip-hop rap phenomenon that has been a factor in youth dialect bands in Italy. On another level, he also goes on to discuss in detail many Canadian and American Italian writers who address not the separation between black and white or the simplistic bipolar Canadian cultural war between the French and British, but the connections that we share culturally and socially.

Verdicchio's work is one of the most important studies that has been published on Italian emigration and North American Italian culture in recent years. It anticipates all the works on Italians and race that have been published over the last fifteen years. The work challenges stereotypical, racist notions about southern Italians. He demonstrates how these same racist attitudes have influenced the status of all Italians, including their offspring in both Canada and America. His work helps us to understand better that complex ethnic Italian identity in its relationship historically to Italy and in its reconstruction in North America. Most important of all, he challenges convincingly the boundaries that separate ethnic groups both nationally and internationally and demonstrates that Italians in the Diaspora and Italians in Italy are, indeed, "bound by distance".

Works Cited

D'Alfonso, Antonio. *In Italics*. Toronto: Guernica, 1996.

Tuzi, Marino. "Writing the Minority Subject." *The Anthology of Italian-Canadian Writing*. Ed. Joseph Pivato. Toronto: Guernica, 1998. 360-366.

Verdicchio, Pasquale. *Approaches to Absence*. Toronto: Guernica, 1994.

_____. *Devils in Paradise: Writings on Post-Emigrant Cultures*. Toronto: Guernica, 1997.

_____. *Moving Landscape*. Montréal: Guernica, 1985.

_____. *Nomadic Trajectory*. Montréal: Guernica, 1990.

_____. *The House Is Past: Poems 1978-1998*. Guernica, 2000.

LAURA E. RUBERTO

UNRAVELING *BOUND BY DISTANCE*: VERDICCHIO'S THEORY OF SUBALTERNITY

IN THE PREFACE, Pasquale Verdicchio explains that one of the main aims of the book "is to challenge the kind of thinking that reproduces the 'West' as a stable and homogenous political and discursive entity." He uses the example of Italy, with its unique history of migration and social and political unrest, to discuss contemporary critical theories of nationalism, race, class, and gender in relation to the production of culture. In particular, Verdicchio engages a wide range of contemporary cultural critics — Stuart Hall, Gayatri Spivak, Ernesto Laclau, and Chantal Mouffe, to name a few — in his effort to critique the re-production of East/West binaries. Through a careful reading of cultural texts he forms a kind of theory of subalternity.

This book contributes to recent cultural studies approaches to the disciplines of Italian and Italian-American studies for two significant reasons. First, Verdicchio explains why an examination of Italian culture should go hand in hand with a discussion of Italian-American culture. He argues for this connection through an historical reading of the reasons for emigration from and within Italy, the still visible tensions between northern and southern Italy, the past and present situation of Italian immigrants in North America, and the status of immigrants in Italy today. The second trait of Verdicchio's book that stands out is his use of the work of the Italian Marxist thinker, Antonio Gramsci. Taking his cue from Pier Paolo Pasolini, Verdicchio suggests a "new way of being Gramscian". He notes the different ways in which U.S.A. and England-based scholars have used Gramsci, sometimes in a somewhat disjointed or incomplete manner. (One reason for this problem, Verdicchio notes, is the lack of English translations of Gramsci's prison notebooks, a problem now remedied by Columbia University Press.) In addition, he explains the different ways Gramsci has been "neglected" by the Italian intellectual left and at times appropriated, for reactionary purposes, by the Italian right. Verdicchio hopes to recuperate Gramsci for materialist interventions within a cultural studies framework.

Bound by Distance is most interesting and innovative when it points to the hybridity inherent in any creative cultural text. This intricate analysis perhaps comes through best in Chapters Three and Four when Verdicchio speaks directly about migrant communities in Italy and North America and their artistic output, but it is nonetheless apparent throughout.

In Chapter One, "The South as Dissonant National Subject", Verdicchio considers the racialized distinctions between northern and southern Italians created through nationalist discourses, differences that have historically reinforced an anti-southern prejudice. Furthermore, by looking at the manifold ways in which southerners were represented discursively by various politicians and intellectuals interested in Italian unification, he successfully argues that the Italian Risorgimento was founded and energized by a kind of colonialist mission. He traces the ever-present question of language and the construction of a unified, national identity through readings of Dante, Petrarca, Ippolito Nievo, Giovanni Pascoli, and Enrico Corradini. In the end, what makes the chapter's historical argument and close readings so important is the illustration of the reasons why these issues remain significant today to anyone invested in Italian culture and politics.

Chapter Two, "The Subaltern Written/The Subaltern Writing: Standing Figurations of Southern Cultural Expression", considers the definition of "subaltern writing" and problematizes representations of the subaltern. Continuing from his earlier discussion of racial prejudices against southerners developed out of the discourse of unification, Verdicchio here focuses specifically on long-standing Neapolitan stereotypes. The book's interdisciplinarity comes through in this chapter's presentation of an amalgam of creative expressions and cultural theories. Thus, we encounter a rich dialogue on the following: the representation of subalterns in film (specifically in the films of Elvira Notari) and in literature (in the writing of Pasolini); consumerism and the use of stereotypes (in the best seller and film adaptation of *Io, speriamo che me la cavo*); and the relationship between pedagogy and the ability of the subaltern to express him/herself outside of stereotypes (engaging Giroux's notion of "critical pedagogy" and Spivak's question "Can the subaltern speak?").

Verdicchio links Chapter Three, "Bound by Distance: The Italian Immigrant as Decontextualized Subaltern", by a discussion of Italian-American (U.S.) and Italian-Canadian cultural expressions, and yet it is much more than merely a literary critic's musings. In fact, he begins, in what is his strongest chapter, by taking to task Italianists who study "literature of emigration" in a rather single-minded way. These critics distinguish between a kind of "high" Italian culture, produced by an Italian living in a self-imposed "exile" in North America and writing in Italian, and the literary output of Italian immigrants (of any generation), often writing in English and/or in an Italian dialect.

Verdicchio questions the belief that an Italian literature of emigration must be written in Italian, urging inclusion of Italian immigrant writers regardless of the language in which they write. He then moves on to a study of various representations of and productions by artists of the Italian Diaspora (or what Verdicchio calls "decontextualized subalterns"). Indeed, one of the most interesting critiques in *Bound by Distance* is the examination of Spike Lee's use of Italian-American characters in *Jungle Fever* and *Do the Right Thing*, figures who help to illustrate the intricacies of racial and ethnic tensions/solidarities in the United States. The chapter closes with a review of Italian-Canadian and Italian-American writers. He looks at the term "multicultural" with respect to both specific Italian-Canadian writers and the Association of Italian Canadian Writers. Further, he considers how racial and ethnic identities (specifically, southern Italian American and Sicilian American identities) intersect with lesbian identities, and how both are written into the poetry and fiction of two Italian-American women authors, Rose Romano and Dodici Azapadu.

Chapter Four, "A New Way of Being Gramscian", rounds out the book nicely by returning to the Italian landscape for a look at different ways in which marginal voices have spoken in film, popular music, literature, and political activism in twentieth century Italy. While Verdicchio's reading of Gramsci's work informs the entire book, it is here in Chapter Four that he details the complexities of Gramsci's thought. The chapter focuses on Gramsci's pre-prison essay, "Some Notes Regarding the Southern Question", especially in relation to contemporary political paradigms in Italy.

Bound by Distance is a fascinating exercise in contemporary cultural studies. Perhaps the main fault of the book, its ambitiousness, is also its strongest virtue. Verdicchio engages an overwhelming number of primary and secondary texts in a critical, comparative, and cross-disciplinary manner. Such breadth offers much to a critical discourse outside a strictly Italian one.

While the uniting theme of the book is Italian diasporic culture, this interdisciplinary study speaks to a much wider audience. It offers novel interventions into the discourse of nationalism, the consciousness and power of subaltern groups, the racialization of minorities, and the gendering of ethnic stereotypes. More specifically, Verdicchio's thoughts on Lee's films and his study of Italian hiphop and rap (in Chapter Four) provide insightful discussions about the field of African American cultural criticism. And his readings of Romano's and Azapadu's work are careful investigations of how fiction and poetry can work out the knots caused by seemingly conflicting cultural/racial/gender identities. Most importantly, however, Verdicchio offers a much-needed contextualization of the life and work of Antonio Gramsci, a thinker who, as we reach the end of the millennium, continues to be central to any thorough consideration of culture and politics.

ANTONIO D'ALFONSO AND PASQUALE VERDICCHIO

A CONVERSATION

ANTONIO D'ALFONSO: November 18, 2000. Pasquale just published *The House Is Past*, and we will be talking about that book. We're in Montreal at my parents' house, and the camera's rolling.

PASQUALE VERDICCHIO: Welcome to Montreal.

AD: So let's start with the beginning, no, better still, let's start with the end.

PV: Okay. I should get the book.

AD: It's right here.

PV: Here is *The House Is Past*, the collected poems from 1978 to 1998, twenty years of production, which marks both an end and a beginning, because 1998 is the year that I went to Italy for two years; it is a transition period for me. Probably the best place to start would be at the end: the last poem is entitled *Postscript*.

Feet up
thirty-seven thousand feet up
in the air of winter
barely leading a Canadian front
on Ash Wednesday with only return
the real thought inescapable
to where thousands of feet up again
the weather waits
and the weight of flight continues
to make insomnia a thing of the past
merely jet-lagged is slightly tired
language changes in the transition
from state to state to state the obvious
but I mean that language even changes
on the way from mind to mouth
slowed down and slurred
feet up
to get the blood flowing again
down to my head and full circulation
no longer a way out
walking against direction in fuselage
again leaving to return
and return as leaving.

That "walking against direction in fuselage" is a line that was in my mind for years. It's the line that I used to think about as a kid. When we took the plane, because we flew to Vancouver when we left Italy, I was thinking how I could walk down along the plane in the opposite direction that the plane was going to avoid reaching the destination. Finally I got to use it in a poem. So twenty years of working in a language that's borrowed and changed and put together, stitched to other languages, in order to try and make sense of something. I'm not sure what that something is but I guess when you look back on it, something must be said for these words. I don't know.

AD: *Postscript*. Then you have *Terra Mara, Male Diction. Male Diction, Male Diction*.

PV: Yes.

AD: Why that word play?

PV: *Male Diction* I guess, *Postscript* is a part of that series. It's the last series of poems in the book. *Male Diction* because I feel that males have a language of their own that hits up against their maleness; the inability to escape that diction is a *male* (evil) diction because it keeps us from communicating. I really started thinking about that male diction when my daughter was born and how I would try and attempt to communicate to her certain things outside of the influence of my maleness. *Terra Mara* is obviously dedicated to her, her name is Mara, so Terra *Mara* and also the play on words *Terra* Mara.

AD: But Terra Mara also means Italy. . .

PV: Yes.

AD: I like that poem.

PV: The attempt to find a name for it was all related to that sort of looking back and trying to create a connection. All these poems, looking back again after twenty years, make up a history not only of myself, but of the families, a history of the people that I met during these twenty years. It's also my history with you of Guernica, because I started publishing with you. So it traces out that line that goes from 1984 when I first met you and the other Italian-Canadians, in Rome, establishing a sort of relationship; going through the evolution with the association of writers and the struggles within the association; the fights and the attempt to not only write poetry but also essays, trying to get a grasp of this situation that we're living. It becomes a journal of my twenty years before and after the association.

AD: We're talking about extra, extra-curricular activities, in fact. I want to go back to your book because it's also an evolution in style. It's amazing how many styles you have in that book. Whether you start from the beginning, *Moving Landscape* which is more lyrical, to *Nomadic Trajectory* which was, I think, the most interesting in many ways because, structurally, you were changing. But *Approach* is the one where you put everything together.

PV: Mm, hmm.

AD: Now you're moving towards lyricism, I think. Am I right or wrong?

PV: You're right. There's never been actually a straight lyrical or narrative mode. In the beginning, yes, it started with a semi-narrative lyrical form and now in the poetry at the end of *The House Is Past* I've gone back to that form.

AD: There's also a temptation to write prose.

PV: It's more a prose type of writing. All of the writing is experimental in the sense that I'm always looking for a form and I find that in composing any type, even one short poem, I have the ideas, I might have the subject matter and the themes and the metaphors and all that stuff, but before I can actually write, it's the form that really dictates when I begin to write. It's a process of finding a form and the book reflects that. Each segment represented here reflects a period which I found it necessary to find a form that was different from the last one used. So whether it's dictated by readings, interests in whatever another medium, like film or photography, because the visual arts are very influential in my writing. I like them, I use them, I absorb them, I regurgitate them through my writing. They all necessitate a different format. It's an experimental notebook, *The House Is Past*, of the stages in my life where I have approached different aspects of culture, absorbing them, and then re-presented them in my own words, everything passing through the filter of language which continues to be a challenge – coming face-to-face with a foreign language like English, trying to make it mine, trying to maintain my Italian, trying to maintain my dialect.

Then, with children, you begin to hear how language is acquired and that becomes interesting, all the combinations of words that appear, especially when they're working through two languages, Italian and English. I love words that my children came up with and I try to insert those in somewhere. Instead of *luna* for moon, it's *muna*, instead of *fish* and *peixe* it's *peish*. Those are fantastic. I used one in one poem; instead of *nightmare* my son Juliano says *night mirror* which is a good reflection of what we do with dreams and images.

So *Male Diction* is a type of circling back to one's consciousness and awareness of our cultural position and cultural conditioning. *Terra Mara* is an attempt to reconstitute something for my children through rituals which I insert in the poems, rituals associated to Southern Italy.

In *Approaches to Absence,* we're now working backwards through chronology. *Approaches to Absence* is the recounting of all of my work with language and culture. I think most people read *Approaches to Absence* in the opposite sense of what I mean. I don't mean that a silencing or an erasure of myself, an *assimilation*. It's an *absence*, I'm trying to obscure the mechanisms that make my writing or my language different. Trying to make absent the mechanism, trying to make it natural which, of course, only seems natural to me because I'm writing it. It might still appear too obscure but hopefully I am having an influence on how people are reading this work. When people approach my reading they are absorbed into it, and hopefully they come to accept that this is a different language. The absence is that I'm posing the language as something to stand behind and appreciate.

AD: That book is the one that people picked up easily anywhere I would present it. It was very strange, I don't know why. Even when there was *Nomadic* and *Moving Landscape Approaches to Absence* is the book they would pick. You have a nice photograph on the cover. What was it? You have a door I believe.

PV: Yes.

AD: But that's not it. I don't know what it is. It must be the title.

PV: I think that's the one book that people probably know most. If you can say that about *Approaches to Absence*. It might be because it presents also dimensions that are more universal in the sense that there is a lot of spirituality in it. There is a spiritual angle to that book that maybe makes a more direct connection, everything else can flow through. And that spirituality, I don't want to call it, *religion?*, but I'm not referring to organized religion like Catholicism. Obviously it's influenced somewhat by that, and you can see it if you read it. By the spirituality that rose at the time when Mara was born, she was my first child. A reassessment of positions of meaning of one's life as given by this new meaning of one's life. There's quite a bit of spirituality in there. It's a meditative spirituality, a meditation upon new life.

In *Approaches to Absence*, there's just a short poem, "Nothing Can Be Done", which I believe explains this transition of languages, this exciting new way of looking at things.

> And lately my hands have become
> ears for a strange movement
> hardly audible speech of epidermal waves.

That the child in the belly chose these waves of presence... it's amazing to see... to touch... to be in connection with another world and with yourself at the same time.

AD: I did not know that. I did not know that that's what it meant, that poem; so it's about birth.

PV: Pre-birth.

AD: Pre-birth?

PV: Existence in the womb where we all want to go back to. Before *Approaches* there is a small book that I published with Jahbone Press in Los Angeles, *The Posthumous Poet*, which was a series of poems that was, I guess, inspired by my spending a summer at the Pasolini archive in Rome where I got to go through all his papers and see all his films and all the outtakes. It was an amazing experience. The material in there is fantastic and just an incredible archive, photographs, film, everything. After spending a summer reading and viewing films, these poems developed. I was attempting to work on a book on Pasolini which didn't work out. I eventually used that material to write some articles on Pasolini but that experience really manifested itself in a different type of book, not a critical book but a book of poetry, what his work really represented for me. I don't know what to say, he's just a fantastic individual with an incredible influence that has yet to be recognized in Italy. Few understand the impact that he had on Italian culture.

Before *The Posthumous Poet* we go back to *Nomadic Trajectory* which was really a transitional book for me; it encapsulates the linguistic and compositional experimentation that I was trying and that defined itself and made it possible for me to go on and write other books.

AD: They're very different.

PV: Yes, they are.

AD: *The Posthumous Poet* and *Nomadic Trajectory*. I realized that it was very different, a total different experience.

PV: It's hard to say – one of them wasn't me.

AD: Exactly.

PV: But I'm not sure which one wasn't me. I can't tell you which one wasn't me because I needed to do both, but, yes, they are extremely different. One is much more full of emotion, the Pasolini book, while *Nomadic Trajectory* is full of a subterranean emotion. I needed to get out certain forms that would give me freedom. The compositional aspects of *Nomadic Trajectory* do that. It's a very odd composition, it's a very odd book. I chose the image of a desert and a nomad because I needed to establish a virtual territory in which I could move. I had done things with language, form had always been important for me. I had already done things with language and form but now I needed to define my own space within the English language and within poetic form. I'm still not sure if those poems are successful or not; of course, they didn't get reviewed very much. Maybe one can zero in on these forms. I broke the verses up to give a sense of movement point-to-point. You move either down or across to read, whichever way you go you always come up to, you have to face the space that's in between the verses or between the sections, and then every once in a while you hit upon these little pieces that block the way. I was trying to work my way through language and form in that sense.

After having done this, I became not more comfortable, but more . . . I defined form for myself more clearly. It really helped to go through this. I didn't know at the time if it would work and, as I said, it's still not clear; needed to define a territory. For example, there is a poem "Branta canadensis" which is about borders. I had just moved to Los Angeles, then to San Diego; I was near the Mexican border and all of a sudden the border shifted for me. I was once again a sort of immigrant.

Before I was close to the U.S.A. border by being in Vancouver. I shifted down about one thousand miles to be near another border. Everything became virtual, more undecided, more schematic as to where I was and who I was and what I should relate to. In fact, in my first years in California I felt like I was going through an identity crisis. Trying to define myself, I really didn't know if I was American, Canadian, or Italian. At the same time, I was attracted to Mexico, which was a great way for me to define a new culture. Finding Mexico and the desert in California was of paramount importance for my being able to stay there and feel comfortable. Resolving the identity issue I realized that I was nothing.

AD: Nothing?

PV: I'm not a Canadian, I'm not American, I'm not Italian.

AD: You're a man of the world.

PV: I don't know that. That's a different thing. *Parthenope* also is part of that series of poems which is a composition about Naples and the different dimensions that you find in Naples: the pre-Greek, the Greek, the Roman and the contemporary post-Roman period. And everything else that comes with these periods, the various foreign invasions and governments. There is a layering in Naples, my native city, which makes it impossible to really state one's identity one way or another. You can't say "I'm Neapolitan" and mean anything specific because the influences are just too many. How do you find, go back and find who you are?

We have the Arabic, we have the Moorish, we have the Greek, we have the Spanish, we have the Roman, we have all those mixed up together. The culture that exists now is a result of all those. I brought those elements together: the indecision, the undecided, the identity of my shift down to another border, and going back and re-assessing what *Naples*, *Napolis*, and *Napoli* could mean. As I say in the poem, this is not a tautology. There is no direct correspondence between any of them. They are all transition states. That's where I found myself at that time. You have form-wise, composition-wise, thematic, thematics in the book are transitional that led them into *Posthumous* and *Approaches*. Actually more *Approaches* than *Posthumous* because *Posthumous* took a different direction.

Nomadic Trajectory is an odd collection. *Isthmus* I had published in Los Angeles with Littoral Press. It was just after my move to San Diego and this probably is a preview of the forms that I used in *Nomadic Trajectory*. *Isthmus* is a book that I feel less satisfied with because it's an in-between book. I had started that work in *Ipsissima verba* which, to me, is a very strong book in the sense that the statements that I make with language and form have been very important for me.

All of this came after a more narrative book like *Moving Landscape*. So *Ipsissima*, which was a little 16-page pamphlet that I published myself through Parentheses Writing Series, was a switch. It was a click; my working in a new mode. That's why *Isthmus* feels sort of odd. There is a more direct jump from *Ipsissima* to *Nomadic* but there were some things happening in my life at that point that needed to emerge. An isthmus is a piece of land that connects a peninsula or an island; it is a narrow piece of land. I was looking for something I needed to cross from one place to another, and *Isthmus* represents that. It takes me back to my education as a biologist. It has to do with the ocean, the sea, the isotherms, which are layers of different types of waters in the ocean. You have one mass of water that's one temperature of salinity and another mass just underneath it that is another temperature of salinity. The isotherm is a thin line where the two meet. The isthmus is a thin line when one piece of land meets another piece of land. I was trying to meet myself somewhere. I was trying to find that layer in myself. That's why it's an odd book. I found this great image by Clemente from the series of etchings *Napolitano*, which presents two people whose hands are joined to become one arm without hands. That to me also represented the Isthmus, or a conjoining, the uncertainty of where one body begins and the other one ends.

The first book that I published with Guernica, *Moving Landscape*, was begun in 1978 but came out in 1985. There is a large period of silence there. That is why in 1986 *Ipsissima verba* was ready to come out. I don't know if you can talk about poetry books as a necessity, *Isthmus* wasn't necessary as a book, but it was necessary as a writing exploration. I was looking for something.

AD: Didn't that fit in the other book, that poem?

PV: It didn't make sense. It just didn't make sense to me to be with anything else. It was just too strange. Not even *Ipsissima verba* would have fit with *Nomadic Trajectory*. Aside from using form, I think of these poems, even though they might be small and individual, as a block. I'm always working on, not a theme, but issues that define themselves as a block. If you put them together and it seems odd now that they are altogether in one book. They had to come out individually because that's what I was going through at the time. It simply didn't make sense to me to publish them together in one book. *Moving Landscape:* What can I say about *Moving Landscape*? It has taken me a long time to feel comfortable with *Moving Landscape*.

AD: Why?

PV: The poems are early things. I just wasn't sure about myself as a writer, I guess, though I loved the work, if I may be arrogant. The work represents movement, traveling; many of the poems were written in Spain and Mexico, in Italy and Holland. The poems are collected from my moving around so much. That movement enabled me to read outside of what was available to me in Italian as far as the books that I could find in Vancouver. And in the very well-defined and squared off Canadian culture that I was able to meet in Vancouver. Vancouver at that time was very isolated. It is much more cosmopolitan today but at that time it was incredibly isolated, and what existed as culture was very well defined. There was no going outside those limits.

My first inkling, outside of the travel, of something else happening in Canada was when I went to the western front, I don't think it's Hastings but the street just below Hastings, maybe Powell. I went to the Western Front Bookstore and fell on a book by Guernica. I saw an Italian name on a book of poetry in English. It was Filippo Salvatore's.

AD: *Suns of Darkness.*

PV: *Suns of Darkness.* I saw that there was something that clicked in me. What that was all about? *Moving Landscape* eventually came out of, meeting of these other people, and meeting with you, Antonio. Because really, my experience as a writer up to that point in Vancouver and Victoria didn't feel like it had an out. I had taken workshops at the University of Victoria while I was studying there. I was working in the library, took workshops with Robin Skelton with his incredible knowledge of literature and writing. Yet I could never find a connection with the other writers and often couldn't find a connection with the people who were leading the workshops. *Moving Landscape* represents that period of not having connections, trying to find connections, eventually seeing that something else outside existed and attempting to make that leap outside of Vancouver to that somewhere else.

AD: What was that "somewhere else"?

PV: I wrote a sonnet à la Leopardi when my uncle died . . . then in English I started using puns, using my biology learned terminology, writing about tape-worms, stuff influenced by John Lennon's writings. There was a book of his drawings and writings that came out, I don't remember the title. Do you remember the title, Antonio?

AD: *A Spaniard in the Works.*

PV: That's right. I started imitating him because that seemed to be a way to undermine the language and play with the language to get unconventional results that would communicate what I wanted to say. Take language and twist it.

AD: When did you write your first poem? In what year?

PV: I have no idea.

AD: How old were you?

PV: It was sometime ago . . . if we're talking about the English stuff . . .

AD: Yes.

PV: It would be sometime in the mid-1970s.

AD: And the Italian works?

PV: The Italian stuff? I kept a diary when I was nine years old that somebody gave me and I started writing down thoughts.

AD: Do you still have that?

PV: I still have that, yes, but it's nothing special. I'm not one of those who thinks he is a writer . . .

AD: Mozart.

PV: Mozart is completely different. No, but I've always enjoyed words and I've always enjoyed language and intelligent communication either as a possibility or to undermine communication.

BIBLIOGRAPHY

AWARDS

Swiss Ambassador to Canada Book Prize, 1978.

Italian American Cultural Foundation, Educator of the Year Award, 1995.

Multiculturalism Canada Award for *Devils in Paradise*, 1996.

EPA Faculty Exchange Award, Univ. of Bologna, 2005. Italian Ministry of culture Translation Award for Andrea Zanzotto's *Fosfeni*, 2009.

Bressani Prize for Poetry for *This Nothing's Place*. 2010.

Visiting Fellow, University of Warwick Center for Advanced Studies, UK 2011.

POETRY BOOKS

Moving Landscape. Montreal: Guernica, 1985.

Ipsissima Verba. Los Angeles: Parentheses, 1986.

A Critical Geography. Illustrations by Italo Scanga. San Diego: Parentheses, 1989.

Nomadic Trajectory. Montreal: Guernica, 1990.

Isthmus. Los Angeles: Littoral Editions, 1991.

The Posthumous Poet: A Suite for Pier Paolo Pasolini. Los Angeles: Jahbone Press, 1993.

Approaches to Absence. Toronto: Guernica, 1994.

The House Is Past. Poems 1978-1989. Toronto: Guernica, 2000.

La nave del mondo. Limited edition. *Gnams Edizioni Artigianali Numerate*. Bologna, Italy. 2000.

Le Paysage qui bouge. Selections from *Moving Landscape* and selected other publications. Translated and with an introduction by Antonio D'Alfonso. Montreal: *Éditions du Noiroît,* 2000.

Object Lessons. Vancouver: Parentheses, 2008.

This Nothing's Place. Toronto: Guernica, 2008.

CRITICAL BOOKS

Futurism and Advertising: Depero Fortunato. With preface. Chapbook. San Diego: Parentheses, 1990.

Bound by Distance: Rethinking Nationalism Through the Italian Diaspora. Madison: Fairleigh Dickinson University Press, 1997.

Devils in Paradise: Writings on Post-emigrant Cultures. Toronto: Guernica, 1997.

Looters, Photographers, and Thieves: Aspects of Italian Photographic Culture in the Nineteenth and Twentieth Centuries. Madison: Fairleigh Dickinson University Press, 2011.

SELECTED TRANSLATIONS

Porta, Antonio. *Invasions and Other Poems.* With Paul Vangelisti and Anthony Baldry. Includes interview with the poet by Pasquale Verdicchio. San Francisco: Red Hill Press, 1985.

Porta, Antonio. *Passenger.* With introduction. Montreal: Guernica, 1986.

Magone, Francesco. *Cosmogony of An Event.* San Diego: Parentheses, 1988.

Villa, Emilio. With Paul Vangelisti. *Foresta Ultra Naturam/The Forest Beyond Nature: Homage to Emilio Villa*. San Francisco: Red Hill Press, 1989.

Vico, Giambattista. *Tropes, Monsters, and Poetic Transformations*. With introduction. Illustrations by Italo Scanga. San Diego: Parentheses, 1990.

Villa, Emilio. *Seventeen Variations on Proposed Themes for a Pure Phonetic Ideology*. With introduction. San Diego: Parenthesis, 1991.

Caproni, Giorgio. *The Wall of the Earth*. With introduction. Montreal: Guernica, 1992.

Zanzotto, Andrea. Poems in *Sulfur Magazine*. 29 (1991): 145-158.

Gramsci, Antonio. *The Southern Question*. With introduction and annotations. Chicago: Bordighera, 1995.

Merini, Alda. *A Rage of Love*. Toronto: Guernica, 1996.

Pasolini, Pier Paolo. *Desperate Vitality. Una disperata vitalità*. Parentheses, 1996.

Porta, Antonio. *Salomè*. Selections from *La lotta e la vittoria del giardiniere contro il becchino*. San Diego: Parentheses, 1996.

Passolini, Pier Paolo. *The Savage Father*. With postface in volume entitled *The Savage Father: Colonialism as a structure that wants to be another structure*." Toronto: Guernica, 1999.

Porta, Antonio. *Metropolis*. Los Angeles: Green Integer Press, 1999.

Ardizzi, Maria. *Women and Lovers*. Toronto: Guernica, 2000.

Porta, Antonio. *Passenger Selected Poems (1958-1979)*. Second edition with new introduction. Toronto: Guernica, 2000.

Perticarini, Romano. *Ragazzi di ieri*. Vancouver: Ital Press, 2001.

Merini, Alda. *The Holy Land*. Trans. and co-written introduction with Stephanie Jed. Toronto: Guernica, 2002.

Pace, Roberto. *The Dark Man*. Toronto: Guernica, 2005.

Gramsci, Antonio. *The Southern Question*. New edition with new introduction. Toronto: Guernica, 2006.

Villa, Emilio. *"Contenuto figurative."* *AUFGABE*. 7 (Spring 2008): 15-24.

Pasolini, Pier Paolo. *In Danger: A Pasolini Anthology*. Edited by Jack Hirschman. San Francisco: City Lights, 2010.

Zanzotto, Andrea. *Fosfeni*. With introduction. Toronto: Guernica, 2010.

Ledda, Gavino. *Padre Padrone*. Sassari: Edizioni Agave, 2011.

Caproni, Giorgio. *Res amissa*. *Journal of Italian Translation*. 1 (Spring 2006): 202-213.

CONTRIBUTORS

Diego Bastianutti, born in Fiume, Italy, has crossed many borders separating States as well as "states of mind". He is at ease with various languages and cultures. After a stint in international banking on Wall Street, he took up his tenure as Professor of Spanish and Italian literature at Queens University from 1970 to 1997, while holding the post of Honorary Vice Consul of Italy (1977-1995). He retired to Sicily with his wife Giusy Oddo, where he spearheaded a movement for the integration and assimilation of new immigrants from Africa and the Middle East. In the last twenty-five years he has had a number of works published, among them *A Major Selection of the Poetry of Giuseppe Ungaretti* (Exile Editions, Toronto 1997), winner of the "1998 John Glassco Prize"; his third poetry collection, *For a Fistful of Soil / Per un pugno di terra (Zeisciu, Milano 2006)* winner of the *2008 International Literary Prize Scritture di frontiera* in Trieste, Italy. *Lost in Transit* (2018) and *The Lotus Eaters/ I mangiatori di loto* (Legas, 2019) are his latest collections of poetry. An anthology of his poetry in Spanish is forthcoming in Havana, Cuba. His prize-winning poems and short stories have been featured in various literary journals and anthologies in the Americas and in Europe. He resides in Vancouver with his wife.

Leonardo Buonomo teaches American Literature at the University of Trieste, Italy. He is the author of *Backward Glances: Exploring Italy, Reinterpreting America (1831-1866)* (Fairleigh Dickinson Univ. Press, 1996) and *From Pioneer to Nomad: Essays on Italian North American Writing* (Guernica, 2003). His most recent publications include "Alla conquista del West: il diario di Sister Blandina Segale" in *Sorelle d'oltre oceano: Religiose italiane ed emigrazione negli Stati Uniti: una storia da scoprire*, ed by Maria Susanna Garroni (Carocci, 2008), "Listening to New York in *The American Scene*" in *Tracing Henry James,* ed. by Melanie H. Ross and Greg W. Zacharias (Cambridge Scholars Publishing, 2008), "Raccontare la capitale: Roma negli scritti di Francis Marion Crawford e Constance Fenimore Woolson" in *Le relazioni tra Stati Uniti e Italia nel periodo di Roma capitale*, ed by Daniele Fiorentino e Matteo Sanfilippo (Gangemi, 2008), and "Six Feet Under: la morte è di casa" in *I Soprano e gli altri: i serial televisivi americani in Italia*, ed by Donatella Izzo e Cinzia Scarpino, *Ácoma* 36 (2008). "The Legacy of John Fante" and "Indovina chi viene a cena? La rappresentazione degli afroamericani nel doppiaggio italiano di *The Jeffersons*" are forthcoming.

Antonio D'Alfonso founded Guernica Editions in 1978. He has published over fifty books and has translated many Quebecois poets of his generation. His poetry has been published in various countries. His novels won the following awards: *Fabrizio's Passion*, the Bressani Award (2000); *Un vendredi du mois d'août*, the Ontario Trillium Award (2005); *L'Aimé* the Christine Dimitriu Van Saanen Award (2008). His feature film, *Bruco,* won two awards at the New York Independent Film Festival, the Best Foreign Film and Best International Director of a Feature film (2010). He holds a Ph.D. from the University of Toronto. In 2016, he received a Honorary Doctorate from Athabasca University. *Two-Headed Man: Collected Poems 1970-2020* was published by Guernica Editions in 2020. He released his fifth feature, *Tata,* in 2020.

Giuliana Gardellini holds a Ph.D. in English and American Studies from the University of Venice. She had a three-year fellowship (2006-2009) in North American Literature at the University of Bologna where she has been lecturer at the Faculty of Foreign Languages and Literatures since 2008. Among her most recent publications, "Riddle and Hermeneutical Quest in *Noman's Land* by Gwendolyn MacEwen" in *Open Letter*, Spring 2007 and, with G. Franci, "From the Adriatic to the Atlantic: Migration and Cultural Identity between Italy and Canada" in *Lingue, leggi e libri da una costa all'altra. Migrazioni (e navigazioni) di uomini e idee*, ed. by L. Michelacci and E. Musiani. (CLUEB, 2007).

Carmelo Militano is a poet and prose writer. His latest work is *Lost Aria,* a short story collection. His biography of Amedeo Modigliani, *Catching Desire,* published in 2019 by Ekstasis Editions.

Joseph Pivato, Professor of Literary Studies at Athabasca University (Edmonton), has focused his research and teaching on Italian-Canadian writing. His publications include *Contrasts: Comparative Essays on Italian-Canadian Writing* (Guernica, 1985 & 1991) and *Echo: Essays on Other Literatures* (Guernica, 1994 & 2003). He is the editor of *The Anthology of Italian-Canadian Writing* (Guernica, 1998), *F.G. Paci: Essays on His Works* (Guernica, 2003), *Caterina Edwards: Essays on Her Works* (Guernica, 2000), *Literatures of Lesser Diffusion* (Univ. of Alberta, 1990), *Mary di Michele: Essays on Her Works* (Guernica, 2007), and *Pier Giorgio Di Cicco: Essays on His Works* (Guernica, 2011). He was born in Italy, lived in Toronto, and earned a Ph.D. from the University of Alberta. See his website: http://mais.athabasscau.ca/faculty /jpivato

Laura E. Ruberto is co-chair of the Department of Arts and Cultural Studies at Berkeley City College. She is the author of *Gramsci, Migration, and the Representation of Women's Work* (Rowman & Littlefield, 2007/2010), the co-editor of *Italian Neorealism and Global Cinema* (Wayne State University Press, 2007), and the translator of *Such Is Life, Ma la vita e' fatta cosi: A Memoir* (Bordighera, 2010). A Fulbright Faculty Research Scholar, she also co-edits the book series "Critical Studies in Italian America" at Fordham University Press and is the Film and Digital Media Review Editor for the *Italian American Review*. She keeps a blog, "*Raccogli e Passa*: Dispatches from California," at i-italy.org.

Ken Scambray has published *A Varied Harvest: The Life and Works of Henry Blake Fuller*, University Pittsburgh Press. 1987; *The North American Italian Renaissance: Italian Writing in America and Canada*, Guernica, 2000; *Surface Roots: Stories.* Guernica, 2004. *Queen Calafia's Paradise: California and the Italian American Novel*, Fairleigh Dickinson University Press, 2007.

Anna Zampieri Pan, born in Vincenza, Italy, is a journalist. She moved to Vancouver, British Columbia, in the 1980s and continued to work as a journalist with the newspaper *L'Eco d'Italia,* and many other Italian language papers in North America dedicating herself to the problems of immigration.

Pasquale Verdicchio, one of the founders of the Association of Italian Canadian Writers, has taught literature, film, cultural studies, and environmental literature in the Department of Literature at the University of California, San Diego, since 1986. His poetry, essays, and translations from the Italian have appeared with various publishers. His poetry collection, *This Nothing's Place* (Guernica Editions), was awarded the Bressani Prize in 2010. Over the years, he had dedicated himself to the study of Mediterranean migrations. In 2015, he was awarded the 2015 Muir Environmental Fellowship by Muir College, UCSD.

"The road is long, from the streets of Naples, Italy, to the forested shores of British Columbia. I remember it like it was yesterday, my arrival in Vancouver, Canada at the end of the 1960s. Being driven through the city, through Stanley Park, toward the North Shore, with its mountains and vast expanse of forests. It was the first time that the idea of nature had struck me as most emphatically real. It was not only what I had read about, something outside of ourselves, or a place that we might merely visit, but something which envelops us and from which we cannot wholly separate. And so it was with the new language that I would encounter: English. It too, at first foreign and distant but, with time, something that would envelop my life. It would take a while before my young self could find the way to express these new sensations, until my English language skills would allow me to discover the appropriate terms by which to speak and write. Language helped me in my attempt to subvert and express the very discomfort I had initially felt as an outsider. I had to work my way through the 'mythology' of living in Canada, and the actual labour of functioning in its reality. The reality of living was starkly different from the mythological referents I had accumulated before arrival, and from the colonizer population within that environment. In order to make heads and tails of this, poetry unveiled a path that has proved over the years to be fruitful and frustrating, enlightening and obfuscating, and unendingly rewarding" — Pasquale Verdicchio.